BODY WISDOM THROUGH SOUND THERAPY

Discover the Science of Frequency to Relax and Refocus Your Mind and Body, Improve Mental Clarity, Boost Vitality, and Enhance Nervous System Regulation

Grace Bailey

Published by Bailey Premier Publishing LLC

Canadian, Texas 79014

ISBN 978-1-966543-06-0 Paperback
ISBN 978-1-966543-07-7 (Kindle/Epub)
ISBN 978-1-966543-08-4 Hardback
ISBN 978-1-966543-09-1 Audio

Disclaimer:

The author is not a licensed or certified practitioner of Somatic Therapy. The exercises and practices shared in this book are based on personal experience and the positive results achieved through their use. This book is intended for educational and informational purposes only and should not be considered professional medical or therapeutic advice. Please consult a licensed healthcare professional before beginning any new therapeutic or exercise regimen, especially if you have any medical conditions or concerns.

Legal Notice:

The author and publisher of this book disclaim any liability for any injury, loss, or damage resulting from the use or misuse of the information contained within. The content provided is not a substitute for professional care, and all readers are encouraged to seek advice from a qualified healthcare provider. By using the exercises and information in this book, you acknowledge that you are participating at your own risk and accept full responsibility for any outcomes.

CONTENTS

INTRODUCTION

WELCOME TO BOOK 2 of the Body Wisdom series! In *Body Wisdom Through Somatic Therapy*, I shared a glimpse into my journey of holistic healing. This book provides a deeper exploration of the profound role that sound has played in that journey.

As I mentioned in Book 1, I come from a traditional Christian background. I was raised in the church and have attended various congregations throughout my life, experiencing many rewarding and miraculous spiritual encounters. Yet, over time, I couldn't shake the feeling that something was missing. I developed an intense hunger to experience more of the supernatural realm described in Scripture—something often missing in today's traditional churches.

This longing led me to explore new avenues of healing and spirituality, one of which was the power of sound. You may be wondering: What role did sound play in my journey? It all began several years ago when I discovered *Wholetones*. As I listened to its music and learned about Michael Tyrrell's journey, I was introduced to the profound impact of musical frequencies.

Before that, I had never made the connection between music and frequency. I had always been curious about why certain pitches could cause a glass to shatter, but I had never explored the science behind it. When I learned how matching a musical frequency to the natural frequency of an object could influence it, everything started to make sense.

Since then, I have also discovered that every cell in our body vibrates at a specific frequency, and when that frequency is disrupted, "dis-ease" can occur. By using music or specific sounds to deliver the correct frequencies, we can help restore the body to its natural balance and optimal function.

Michael Tyrrell's discovery of *Wholetones* is a fascinating journey that I encourage everyone to explore. You can visit www.wholetones.com to listen to the tracks and find his book, where he shares his remarkable story.

These revelations helped me understand why certain music has had such a powerful impact on my life. Sometimes, just a single note in a song could stir deep emotions within me. One such song that marked the beginning of my sabbatical journey was "Call Me" by Will Reagan of United Pursuit on the album *Found*. This song is a heartfelt prayer with the theme, "Call me out from where I've been." I can confidently say that this prayer was answered in my life, and the impact of sound in my life has only deepened throughout this journey.

Sound healing is a remarkable tool that harnesses the power of vibrations to promote relaxation, reduce stress, and enhance overall well-being. By tapping into the science of frequency, we can create meaningful shifts in our mental, emotional, and physical states. This book is designed to guide you through the fascinating world of sound healing, providing you with the knowledge and practical tools to incorporate this transformative practice into your daily life.

Whether you're a busy professional seeking a moment of calm, a parent looking to create a more harmonious household, or simply someone searching for a deeper connection to yourself, this book is for you. Together, we'll explore the rich history and scientific underpinnings of sound healing, from ancient traditions to cutting-edge research. You'll discover how sound can influence your brainwaves, regulate your nervous system, and promote a greater sense of balance and vitality.

I know firsthand how challenging it can be to prioritize self-care in our fast-paced world. That's why I've designed this book to be accessible and practical, offering simple yet effective exercises and techniques that you can easily integrate into your daily routine. No matter how busy or overwhelmed you may feel, there is always room for a little sound healing magic.

Throughout these pages, you'll find a wealth of information and inspiration, from the basics of sound healing to more advanced practices. We'll explore the power of different instruments, such as tuning forks, singing bowls, and even your own voice. You'll learn how to create a personalized sound healing sanctuary, whether a dedicated space in your home or a peaceful corner of your mind.

As we begin this journey together, I encourage you to approach each chapter with an open heart and a curious mind. Allow yourself to experiment with the practices and find what resonates with you. Trust in the wisdom of your body and the power of sound to guide you toward greater harmony and happiness.

By the end of this book, you'll have a solid foundation in sound healing and a toolkit of practices to help you navigate life's challenges with greater ease and resilience. You'll discover how to tap into the power of frequency to quiet your mind, soothe your soul, and awaken your inner healer.

So, my friend, are you ready to begin this incredible transformation? To unlock the secrets of sound and rediscover the vibrant, balanced life you deserve? Let's dive in together and explore the incredible world of sound healing. Your path to greater well-being starts now, one vibration at a time.

Chapter 1

FOUNDATIONS OF SOUND HEALING

*If you want to find the secrets of the universe,
think in terms of energy, frequency, and vibration.*

–NIKOLA TESLA

HAVE YOU EVER WALKED into a room where music played softly in the background and felt an immediate calm wash over you? Or perhaps you've experienced goosebumps on your skin when a powerful piece of music hits the perfect note. These experiences aren't just your imagination; they're your body responding to the profound power of sound. This chapter introduces the foundation of sound healing—an ancient practice that has been around for centuries and still finds its relevance in our modern world. We'll explore the roots of sound healing across different cultures and uncover how these practices have evolved, forming the basis of what we now know as sound therapy.

The Ancient Art of Sound Healing: A Historical Overview

Let's start our journey by traveling back in time to the snow-capped mountains of Tibet, where the resonant tones of singing bowls have been a staple in spiritual practices for thousands of years. These bowls, crafted from a unique seven-metal alloy, are not just musical instruments—they are considered sacred. Each metal corresponds to a specific heavenly body and chakra, forming a harmonious link between the cosmos and the human body. Tibetan monks have long

used these bowls in meditation; their soothing sounds are believed to bring tranquility and introspection. The tradition of making these bowls is a closely guarded secret, passed down through generations, and still practiced today by skilled artisans in Nepal's Kathmandu Valley.

In Australia's arid landscapes, the didgeridoo—a long, wooden instrument played by Indigenous Australians—creates a deep, rhythmic drone used for healing and ceremonial purposes. The sound mimics the earth's heartbeat, fostering a profound connection between the player and nature. This instrument offers more than just music; it provides a rhythmic pulse that guides the mind into a meditative state, facilitating mental clarity and emotional healing.

Across the vast stretches of India, Vedic chants have echoed through temples and homes for millennia. These sacred chants, carried on the breath, are believed to have transformative powers. Their vibrations can cleanse the soul and align energies. The ancient texts describe how these chants, when recited with precision, can invoke the divine and promote spiritual awakening. Their rhythmic patterns and melodic tones create a sense of balance and peace, deepening one's connection with the universe.

Native American wooden flutes, crafted with care and precision, are also integral to sound healing. These flutes produce hauntingly beautiful melodies used in rituals to connect the physical and spiritual realms. The music of these flutes is often spontaneous, with each note and melody reflecting the player's inner state. When used in healing ceremonies, the sound of the flute is believed to carry prayers to the heavens, bridging the gap between the earthly and the divine.

Sound has always been an integral part of healing rituals. Rhythmic drumming, for instance, is a practice used by various cultures to induce trance states and promote healing. The rhythmic beat of the drum acts as a guide, leading participants into altered states of consciousness where healing and transformation can occur. Similarly, Gregorian chants, with their harmonious tones, have filled the halls of monasteries for centuries, believed to uplift the spirit and soothe the soul.

Today, we see a seamless transition of these ancient practices into modern sound healing. For example, crystal bowls, often used in wellness centers, echo the principles of their Tibetan counterparts but are made from quartz. They produce pure, ethereal tones that resonate with the body's energy centers, promoting healing and balance. This adaptation shows how ancient wisdom continues to enrich contemporary practices, proving the timeless nature of sound in healing.

The enduring relevance of sound healing is evident in how these practices have stood the test of time, constantly evolving yet maintaining their core principles. Sound, with its ability to transcend language and culture, continues to be a universal tool for healing, offering solace and transformation to those who seek its embrace. As you explore these ancient arts, you'll find that sound healing is not just a practice but a profound journey of self-discovery and connection to the world around you.

Understanding Vibrations: The Science Behind Sound

Why do some sounds make your skin tingle or your heart race? The secret lies in the fascinating world of vibrations. At its core, sound is a series of vibrations that travel through the air, reach our eardrums, and are interpreted by our brains as different tones and pitches. Sound waves consist of frequency, which measures how fast the waves vibrate and is heard as pitch, and amplitude, which is the wave's height and determines volume. To understand frequency, imagine a pebble tossed into a pond—those ripples are much like sound waves, constantly moving and interacting with everything around them.

But how do these waves impact us physically? As many studies have shown, they have an impressive effect on our bodies. When sound waves enter our auditory system, they don't just stop at our ears. They vibrate through our entire body, influencing our brainwave patterns. This process, known as entrainment, helps synchronize our brain's natural rhythms with the sound's frequency, which can lead to changes in our mental state. For instance, specific frequencies can calm the mind, encouraging relaxation and focus, while others can energize and invigorate us. Think of these frequencies as different radio stations—each offering a unique experience.

Fascinatingly, our cells also respond to sound. Vibrations can stimulate cellular activity, promoting healing and regeneration, which explains why plants react positively or negatively to exposure to vibrations. Researchers have found that sound can even influence the autonomic nervous system, which controls many unconscious bodily functions like heart rate and digestion. The right sounds stimulate the parasympathetic nervous system—the part of the body responsible for rest and relaxation—helping you feel calm and centered.

Entrainment is not just a cool trick sound plays on our brainwaves; it's a natural phenomenon that can be observed in many aspects of life. You see it when fireflies synchronize their flashing lights or when people's footsteps fall into rhythm while walking side by side. Even our heartbeats can entrain themselves to music, speeding up or slowing down to match the tempo. This resonance creates a sense of harmony and alignment, allowing us to feel more connected to ourselves and the world around us.

Vibrational science has exciting and accessible practical applications in healing. Using sound to align our body's natural rhythms can promote emotional balance and physical well-being. Therapeutic settings often incorporate sound to help patients relax, reduce stress, and improve their overall quality of life. Practices like sound baths, where soothing vibrations surround participants, or the use of tuning forks to target specific areas of the body demonstrate how sound can be a powerful ally in healing.

The beauty of sound lies in its simplicity and universality. It doesn't require expensive equipment or specialized knowledge to experience its benefits. Whether it's the gentle hum of a tuning fork, the rhythmic strumming of a guitar, or even the sound of your voice, sound is an accessible tool for anyone looking to enhance their well-being. By tapping into the power of vibrations, we can cultivate a deeper understanding of ourselves and find new ways to live more balanced, harmonious lives.

Sound Frequencies and Their Impact on the Body

Close your eyes and picture yourself in a state of complete ease. Soft, soothing sounds surround you, washing over you like a gentle wave. Your mind surrenders to a deep sense of peace as stress fades away. What you feel is more than just relaxation—it's the magic of sound frequencies. Sound healing often taps into specific frequencies known for their therapeutic effects. One fascinating example is Solfeggio frequencies, a set of tones rooted in Western Christianity and Eastern Indian traditions.

These frequencies are not just numbers on a scale—they resonate deeply with our bodies. Consider 528 Hz, renowned for its calming and transformative effects, often associated with DNA repair and healing. Alternatively, 396 Hz is known to help release fear and anxiety, fostering a sense of emotional freedom. These tools aren't abstract concepts; they have been used for centuries to promote emotional and physical well-being.

Another intriguing area of sound healing is binaural beats. When you listen to two slightly different frequencies in each ear, your brain creates a third tone—a binaural beat. This phenomenon can influence mental states by aligning with your brainwaves. For instance, delta waves (1–4 Hz) are linked to deep sleep and relaxation, while theta waves (4–8 Hz) promote creativity and meditation. Imagine using these beats to enhance focus and clarity, like a mental tune-up that helps you easily tackle your to-do list. Studies have shown that binaural beats can reduce stress and anxiety, making them a popular choice for those seeking a mental boost without the side effects of caffeine or medication.

Sound frequencies extend beyond relaxation and focus, leading to lasting physiological changes. By modulating brainwave patterns, specific frequencies can encourage the production of hormones that help reduce stress and promote relaxation, like serotonin and dopamine. This is why many people turn to sound healing to relax after a long day or to set the stage for a restful night's sleep. The soothing vibrations of a tuning fork can also be incorporated into acupuncture sessions, stimulating specific points in the body to enhance the treatment's effectiveness. One treatment method, known as sound acupuncture, blends ancient practices with modern techniques. During a session, you would lie on an acupuncture table, surrounded by soft, soothing sounds—each frequency carefully selected to support your body's healing process.

Despite their many benefits, sound frequencies are often misunderstood. Some dismiss them as just another passing trend or believe their effects are purely placebo. However, science tells a different story. Research has shown that sound profoundly influences our mental and physical states. It doesn't just offer temporary relaxation—it fosters lasting changes in our health and well-being.

Understanding and embracing the power of sound frequencies unlocks a valuable and accessible path to healing. Try integrating sound frequencies into your daily routine to experience their full impact. Whether you listen to a frequency playlist during your commute or unwind with a sound bath at the end of the day, these practices can help you harness the therapeutic power of sound.

As you explore different frequencies, some will resonate more than others. This will be your body's way of guiding you toward what it needs, a gentle reminder that healing is a deeply personal experience. So, let the sound be your guide as you explore the fascinating world of frequencies and their remarkable ability to heal and transform.

The Role of Resonance in Healing

If you've ever felt the deep, comforting rumble of a bass note reverberating through your chest or the tingling sensation of a high-pitched tone dancing along your skin, you've experienced resonance firsthand. In the realm of sound healing, resonance is the phenomenon where sound waves amplify when they match the natural frequency of an object or body. Think of it as a sympathetic vibration—a sort of cosmic harmony where everything aligns, doubling the impact of the sound. In therapeutic settings, resonance amplifies the healing potential of sound, making it a powerful tool for emotional and physical well-being.

The gong bath is a powerful demonstration of resonance at work. First, you lie on a mat, surrounded by gongs of various sizes. As the gongs are struck, they release deep, layered vibrations. The air fills with a symphony of sound waves, creating a deeply immersive and meditative experience. These waves wash over you, penetrating deep into your body and mind. The rich, multidimensional tones of the gongs create a resonant field that encourages relaxation and emotional release. This environment allows individuals to release stress and tension, often resulting in profound peace and clarity. This experience transcends listening; it involves feeling the vibrations move through you, clearing blockages and promoting balance.

The connection between resonance and emotional release is fascinating. Sound waves can unlock pent-up emotions, facilitating catharsis when they resonate with your body's natural frequencies. It's as if the sound gives your emotions a voice, allowing them to surface and be expressed. This process can lead to significant emotional breakthroughs. A friend once shared how, during a sound healing session, the resonant notes of a singing bowl triggered a deep sense of grief she hadn't confronted in years. Tears flowed freely as the sound waves enveloped her, leaving her feeling lighter and more at peace.

In sound healing, various tools and techniques can leverage the power of resonance. Instruments like tuning forks are particularly effective, as they target specific areas of the body, helping to realign energetic imbalances. When struck, these forks emit precise frequencies that resonate with particular parts of the body, promoting healing at a cellular level. The beauty of these tools lies in their simplicity and precision, offering a direct path to resonance. Another method involves vocal toning, where you use your voice to produce a sound that resonates with your body, creating a personalized healing experience.

To enhance the power of resonance in your sound healing practice, start by creating the right environment. Select a quiet, comfortable space where sound can move freely without distractions. Explore different instruments to find the ones that resonate most with you—whether it's the grounding beat of a drum or the delicate chime of a crystal bowl, each carries its unique vibration. By immersing yourself in these sounds, you can deepen your healing experience, allowing the vibrations to guide you toward balance and harmony.

Mind-Body Connection: Bridging Science and Spirituality

Sound healing is more than just a pleasant auditory experience—it harmonizes the deep connection between your mind, body, and spirit. Picture yourself quietly resting as soothing vibrations wash over you, each tone gently flowing through your energy field. This practice transcends mere sound; it's a journey of resonance, where the chime of a singing bowl or the vibration of a tuning fork isn't just perceived by your ears but deeply felt within. It's like a warm embrace that aligns your thoughts, calms your emotions, and energizes your spirit.

The spiritual side of sound meditation is where the magic truly happens. Think of it as a bridge, linking the physical with the ethereal, creating a path to walk freely between the two realms. In this state, mindfulness becomes almost effortless as sounds guide your focus, each vibration gently nudging you toward the present moment. Sound meditation acts as a light that illuminates your inner self and reveals insights hidden beneath the surface. This isn't just meditation; it's a spiritual journey where every sound is a step toward greater awareness.

But let's not forget the science. The mind-body connection through sound is more than just a poetic idea; it's backed by research. Studies show that sound can reduce stress, lower blood pressure, and improve emotional regulation. The vibrations influence our nervous system, encouraging the release of feel-good hormones like serotonin and endorphins. Imagine sound as a gentle massage for your brain, easing the tension and leaving you refreshed. It's a dance between the scientific and the spiritual, where each step leads to a deeper understanding of yourself and the world around you.

There's something incredibly spiritual about balancing your chakras with sound. Each chakra resonates with specific frequencies; when harmonized, you feel aligned and grounded. It's as if the energy centers in your body are notes in a symphony, each playing its part in creating a harmonious whole. This balance helps you feel good; it also connects you with your true self so you can find clarity and purpose. Sound deepens meditation practices, transforming them from moments of quiet reflection into profound explorations of the soul.

Exploring your mind-body connection with sound is a deeply personal adventure.

Start by finding a quiet space to listen to a singing bowl's gentle tones or a mantra's rhythmic hum. Close your eyes and let the sounds guide you. Notice how your body feels, where the vibrations resonate, and what emotions surface. The purpose of this practice isn't to achieve a specific outcome; it's to listen to what your body and spirit have to communicate. Try journaling afterward, capturing insights and feelings that arose during your session. These reflections can be powerful, revealing patterns and opening doors to personal growth.

As you continue exploring the mind-body connection through sound, you'll find that the lines between science and spirituality blur. Sound healing offers a space where both can coexist, each enhancing the other.

It invites you to embrace the mystery of your existence, finding beauty in the unknown. It's a reminder that you are a complex, beautiful being capable of profound transformation. Sound isn't just something you hear; it's an experience that invites you to connect with the deepest parts of yourself, exploring the dance between mind and spirit. As you continue, may the sounds guide you to a place of peace and balance, where the echoes of the past harmonize with the present, creating a melody that is uniquely yours.

Chapter 2

SCIENTIFIC INSIGHTS INTO
SOUND HEALING

Sound will be the medicine of the future.

–EDGAR CAYCE

HAVE YOU EVER WONDERED why a favorite song can lift your mood or how the soothing sounds of nature can instantly relax you? While sound is a pleasant experience for your ears, it's also a powerful tool for healing and wellness. In recent years, the medical community has been exploring the science behind sound therapy, uncovering fascinating insights into its therapeutic potential. From chronic pain relief to postoperative recovery, sound healing is making waves in modern medicine. Let's dive into the research and see how sound is transforming healthcare.

Sound healing has found its place in modern medicine, with clinical studies showcasing its effectiveness in managing chronic pain. Imagine living with constant pain that medication fails to alleviate. Now, imagine finding relief through something as simple as sound. Research has shown that sound therapy can significantly reduce the perception of pain by altering how our brain processes pain signals. In one study, patients with chronic pain reported a noticeable decrease in discomfort after participating in sound healing sessions. The vibrations from instruments like Tibetan singing bowls and tuning forks interact with our nervous system, helping to alleviate pain and promote relaxation. This is far from a placebo effect; it's a tangible change in how our bodies respond to pain.

But sound healing isn't limited to pain management. Its benefits extend to postoperative recovery as well. After surgery, patients often face physical pain, stress, and anxiety. Sound therapy offers a gentle, noninvasive way to support the healing process. Studies have demonstrated that patients who engage in sound therapy after surgery experience reduced levels of anxiety and improved recovery outcomes. Sound's calming vibrations naturally lower blood pressure and heart rate, creating the perfect setting for healing to take place. Like a comforting melody, they lull your body into deep relaxation and restoration.

To ensure the scientific validity of these findings, researchers employ rigorous methodologies. Double-blind trials, where neither the participants nor the researchers know who is receiving the actual treatment, help eliminate bias and ensure reliable results. Control groups play a crucial role in sound therapy research, establishing a benchmark for evaluation. By comparing results between individuals who receive sound therapy and those who don't, researchers can isolate its specific benefits with greater accuracy. This scientific approach lends credibility to sound healing, positioning it as a legitimate and effective modality within the healthcare system.

The outcomes of these studies are promising, indicating that sound therapy can significantly improve patient quality of life. Participants frequently report a deep sense of relaxation, decreased anxiety, and an improved ability to handle their conditions. These benefits go beyond temporary relief to promote lasting well-being. With growing recognition of its therapeutic potential, sound healing is gradually being incorporated into mainstream medicine, supporting a more integrative approach to healthcare.

For example, palliative care settings incorporate sound therapy to help patients manage pain and improve their quality of life during serious illness. This is a testament to the growing recognition of sound healing's potential to complement traditional medical treatments.

Reflection Section: Exploring Sound's Impact

Take a moment to reflect on your own experiences with sound. How do certain sounds or music affect your mood or physical state? Consider keeping a journal to track your observations. Note any changes in mood, pain levels, or stress after listening to specific sounds or engaging in sound healing practices. This personal exploration can deepen your understanding of sound's impact on your well-being and inspire you to integrate sound healing into your daily life.

The integration of sound healing into modern medicine is an exciting development, offering new avenues for treatment and well-being. As we continue to explore the science behind sound, we open up possibilities for a more harmonious and balanced approach to health. Whether you're seeking relief from chronic pain or looking to enhance your post-operative recovery, sound healing offers a promising path forward.

Neuroplasticity and Sound: How Sound Reshapes the Brain

Imagine your brain as a flexible, ever-evolving landscape, constantly reshaping itself in response to new experiences. This incredible ability is called neuroplasticity. It's how your brain learns new skills, adapts to changes, and recovers from injuries.

Now, think about how sound, something we encounter daily, plays a role in this process. More than a sensory experience, sound is a powerful tool that influences how our brain functions and develops. When we talk about auditory stimuli, we're referring to how sounds can create new pathways in the brain, enhancing its ability to adapt and grow. This adaptability is crucial for learning and memory, making sound an invaluable ally in neuroplasticity.

Research delves into how sound induces neuroplastic changes, offering insights into the brain's adaptability. For instance, studies have shown that music and sound therapy can aid individuals recovering from auditory processing disorders. These disorders can make it challenging for people to process and interpret sounds, affecting their ability to communicate and function effectively. Through structured sound interventions, individuals can retrain their brains to process sounds more accurately, improving their language and communication skills. This research highlights sound's potential to reshape neural pathways, allowing the brain to compensate for impaired areas.

Sound therapy finds its way into brain health through various therapeutic applications. Consider stroke rehabilitation, where sound plays a pivotal role. After a stroke, patients may struggle with speech and motor functions. Sound therapy, often through rhythmic music and beat synchronization, supports neural recovery by stimulating brain regions involved in movement and speech. This stimulation encourages the brain to find new ways to perform tasks, aiding recovery.

Sound exercises also benefit memory retention. Listening to specific sound patterns or music can enhance focus and recall, making them handy tools for boosting cognitive performance.

Looking to the future, the possibilities of sound and neuroplasticity are exciting. As technology advances, so do the methods for sound-based neurotherapy. Imagine using virtual reality to create immersive soundscapes that stimulate brain activity in targeted ways. These experiences could be tailored to individual needs, offering a personalized approach to brain health.

Additionally, researchers are exploring how sound can enhance brain-computer interfaces, creating more seamless integration between humans and technology. These advancements could lead to new ways of interacting with the world, where sound isn't just heard but felt and experienced on a deeper level.

Sound's role in neuroplasticity is a testament to the brain's incredible adaptability. By understanding and utilizing the link between sound and neural transformation, we pave the way for groundbreaking therapies and improved brain health. Whether through recovery from injury or enhancing cognitive function, sound offers a versatile and effective means of supporting brain adaptability.

The future may hold even more groundbreaking discoveries as sound continues to reshape our understanding of the mind and its endless potential.

The Nervous System and Sound Frequencies: A Symbiotic Relationship

Consider the nervous system as the body's command center, a complex network that controls everything from your heartbeat to your breathing and determines how you react to the world around you. Sound is a gentle guide that helps this intricate system find balance.

Sound frequencies interact with the nervous system in fascinating ways, primarily through their ability to activate the parasympathetic nervous system. This part of your autonomic nervous system is like the brakes on a car, slowing things down and promoting rest and relaxation. When you listen to soothing sounds, such as the resonant tones of Tibetan singing bowls or the rhythmic crash of ocean waves, your body naturally relaxes, easing stress and tension. It's as if these sounds whisper to your nervous system, saying, "Take it easy, you've got this."

A growing body of research supports the impact of sound on autonomic nervous functions. Studies have shown that sound therapy can affect heart rate variability, an important measure of your heart's ability to adapt to stress. Heart rate variability provides a window into your body's resilience; higher variability generally means better health and stress management.

Researchers have found that when people engage in sound therapy, their heart rate variability improves. This suggests that sound helps regulate bodily functions and promotes overall well-being. The short-term benefit is feeling better in the moment; the long-term benefit is a body that can handle life's challenges with greater ease.

Sound therapy, once thought of as a wellness trend, has become a recognized tool for supporting the management of nervous system disorders. Sound masking techniques offer relief for those with tinnitus, a condition where individuals hear ringing or buzzing without any external source. By introducing background sounds that shift attention away from the internal noise, sound therapy helps the brain tune out the persistent ringing and reduce the perception of tinnitus.

Similarly, for individuals struggling with anxiety and panic disorders, sound therapy can be a game-changer. The rhythmic tones and vibrations help calm the nervous system, reducing the frequency and intensity of anxiety attacks. It's like having a soothing friend to hold your hand during stressful moments, bringing comfort and calm.

Sound healing offers more than temporary relief—it can gradually build the nervous system's capacity to withstand stress. Through regular practice, sound therapy encourages a more balanced response to challenges, supporting long-term health.

Sound provides your nervous system with a daily workout that strengthens its ability to adapt and respond to life's challenges. Regular exposure to healing frequencies can lower the risk of stress-related illnesses and enhance overall well-being. This practice goes beyond symptom management—it builds a strong foundation of resilience and balance to support you through life's ups and downs.

The symbiosis between sound frequencies and the nervous system is a testament to the body's innate ability to heal and adapt.

As you explore the world of sound healing, consider how it might support your nervous system. Whether seeking relief from chronic conditions or simply looking for a way to unwind, sound offers a gentle yet powerful path to balance and vitality.

Stress Reduction Through Sound: Scientific Perspectives

Stress has a subtle way of settling in before you even notice. It might manifest as stiffness in your shoulders after a demanding day or as a sleepless night when your thoughts refuse to quiet down.

Luckily, sound therapy is gaining attention for its remarkable ability to reduce stress. Scientific studies and research have discovered that sound therapy sessions can significantly drop levels of cortisol, the "stress hormone," which results in a calmer, emotionally balanced state. Exposure to soothing sounds gives your body a gentle nudge that reminds it to relax.

So, how does sound work this magic on our stress levels? The answer lies in the way sound influences our brainwaves. When stressed, our brainwaves become erratic, mirroring the chaos we feel inside. Sound therapy helps to alter these brainwave patterns, guiding them toward a more relaxed state. Think of it as a lullaby for your brain, coaxing it into a rhythm that promotes calm and focus. This is why people often feel more centered and relaxed after a sound healing session. It's not just the effect of the music; sound therapy creates harmony within our minds.

There are many practical ways to harness sound for stress relief. One great option is guided sound meditation, which involves listening to specially designed soundscapes that promote relaxation and mindfulness.

Following along with the sounds allows your mind to drift into a peaceful state, leaving stress behind. Another effective technique is using ambient soundscapes in the workplace. Having a gentle waterfall or a forest soundscape playing softly in the background as you tackle your tasks can transform a hectic work environment into a more tranquil space, making it easier to manage stress and stay focused.

Sound plays a crucial role in holistic stress management plans. It's not just a standalone tool; it complements other stress-reduction strategies beautifully. Whether you're pairing it with meditation, stretching exercises, or even deep breathing exercises, sound can enhance the effectiveness of these practices.

Starting your day with a few minutes of sound meditation can set a tone of calm and clarity that lasts throughout the day. Listening to soothing sounds in the evening can help release built-up stress and prepare your mind and body for restful sleep. The beauty of sound healing lies in its simplicity and accessibility. You don't need special equipment or training—just press play on a soundtrack and let the vibrations work their magic.

Incorporating sound into your stress management plan can be a game-changer. It offers a gentle reminder to pause, breathe, and let go of the worries that weigh you down. Whether you're dealing with a demanding job, family responsibilities, or just the everyday chaos of life, sound offers a pathway to peace. While exploring sound therapy, you might notice that specific frequencies or tones feel more aligned with you than others. It could be the soothing tones of a singing bowl or the rhythmic beat of a drum. Whatever it is, embrace it as your personal stress-relief tool. Let it guide you to a place of calm and clarity, where stress no longer holds power over you.

The Chemistry of Sound: Hormonal and Cellular Changes

Have you ever noticed how a favorite song can lift your spirits or how the gentle hum of a lullaby can soothe a restless baby to sleep? These experiences are deeper than personal preference or nostalgia; they involve remarkable biochemical processes happening within your body. Sound can influence your hormonal balance, which in turn positively affects your overall health and mood.

When you hear certain sounds, your brain releases endorphins—those feel-good chemicals that create a soothing wave of relaxation, enhancing your mood and easing pain. This natural boost triggers a sense of happiness and well-being.

Dopamine, often dubbed the "pleasure hormone," is also stimulated by sound. Dopamine is involved in reward and motivation pathways in your brain. When you listen to music you love, your brain releases dopamine, which explains why that song can make you feel so good. You are not just enjoying the rhythm or melody; your brain is chemically responding to sound.

Studies highlight how sound therapy can enhance dopamine production, potentially improving mood and promoting a sense of well-being. This biochemical magic reminds us how interconnected our senses and emotions are and how sound can be a powerful ally in maintaining mental health.

Sound also plays a pivotal role in regulating other hormones, like melatonin, which is crucial for sleep. Melatonin is the hormone that tells your body it's time to rest. Research shows that sound therapy can increase melatonin levels, helping you achieve better quality sleep. Think of it as nature's lullaby, guiding you into a peaceful slumber. When you incorporate sound healing into your bedtime routine, you're not just setting the stage for a calm evening; you're actively engaging in a practice that supports your body's natural rhythms, ensuring you wake up refreshed and ready to take on the day.

Beyond hormones, sound influences cellular processes, promoting health and repair at the most fundamental level. Think of your cells as tiny, hardworking factories. When exposed to specific sound frequencies, these factories increase their productivity, promoting regeneration and repair.

Studies highlight that sound can stimulate cell growth and recovery, much like sunlight fuels a growing plant. In addition to healing injuries, it optimizes your body's natural ability to maintain and restore itself.

Research also suggests that sound frequencies can positively influence mitochondrial function—the tiny, energy-producing structures within your cells responsible for generating adenosine triphosphate (ATP), the body's primary energy source, which provides the necessary power for various biological processes, including muscle contraction, nerve signaling, and cellular repair.

Certain frequencies, particularly in the low-frequency and infrasonic ranges, have been found to enhance mitochondrial efficiency by stimulating cellular resonance, reducing oxidative stress, and improving ATP production. This process supports overall vitality, boosts energy levels, and may contribute to cellular repair and longevity.

These biochemical changes don't just happen in isolation; they ripple out, affecting broader health outcomes. Improved hormonal balance and cellular health translate into tangible benefits for your life. You might experience more energy, less stress, and sharper mental focus. Your immune system may become more robust and better equipped to avoid illness.

By embracing sound as a tool for health, you're not just treating symptoms; you're supporting your body's capacity to heal and thrive. This holistic approach recognizes the intricate dance between mind, body, and sound.

Sound healing offers a harmonious blend of ancient wisdom and modern science. By tapping into the biochemical impacts of sound, you're connecting with a practice that nurtures from the inside out. As you explore these soundscapes, consider how they might support your health journey. Whether through music, nature sounds, or guided meditations, remember that every note has the potential to enhance your well-being. This is just the beginning of understanding how profoundly sound can influence your life, both in body and spirit.

A Look at the Controversy of 432 Hz vs. 440 Hz

For centuries, different cultures and musicians used varying tuning standards, often influenced by regional traditions, available instruments, and even personal preferences. Among these, 432 Hz was historically common and is sometimes referred to as "Verdi's A," as the renowned Italian composer Giuseppe Verdi advocated for it. Some believe this frequency is more harmonious with natural vibrations and human biology.

However, by the early 20th century, efforts were made to standardize tuning worldwide. In 1936, the International Standards Organization (SO) recommended 440 Hz as the concert pitch for the musical note A4. This change was officially adopted in 1955 as the global standard and reaffirmed in 1975. The shift was largely driven by orchestras and music industries aiming for uniformity, as well as research that suggested 440 Hz was more practical for modern instruments and performances.

There are claims that the change was influenced by military or propaganda reasons, with some arguing that 440 Hz creates tension and disharmony in the listener, while 432 Hz resonates more naturally with the body's energy field and the Earth's frequency (Schumann Resonance at ~7.83 Hz).

Despite the standardization of 440 Hz, many musicians, sound healers, and alternative music theorists continue to advocate for 432 Hz, believing it has calming and healing effects. Some contemporary artists even retune their instruments to 432 Hz, seeking a more harmonious listening experience.

As a result of this change, the obvious question is whether any studies have determined which frequency is the most beneficial for listeners. The following scientific studies may shed some light on the impact of these two frequencies:

1. **Anxiety reduction in dental patients:**
   A random clinical trial investigated the impact of music tuned to 432 Hz and 440 Hz on patients undergoing tooth extraction. Both frequencies significantly decreased clinical anxiety levels compared to no music. However, the 432 Hz group exhibited a more substantial reduction in salivary cortisol levels, a physiological marker of stress, suggesting a potentially greater calming effect.

2. **Physiological and psychological effects in cancer patients:**
   A recent study assessed the effects of sound interventions tuned to 432 Hz and 440 Hz on cancer patients. Both tunings led to improvements in psychological outcomes, such as reduced anxiety and stress. Notably, the 432 Hz intervention resulted in a more pronounced reduction in heart rate and blood pressure, indicating deeper relaxation.

3. **Stress reduction in emergency nurses:**
   Research involving nurses during the COVID-19 pandemic compared the effects of music tuned to 432 Hz and 440 Hz. Both frequencies effectively reduced anxiety levels, but the 432 Hz tuning showed a more significant decrease in certain physiological stress markers.

4. **General benefits of 432 Hz music:**
   Advocates of 432 Hz tuning claim it offers various benefits including stress reduction, improved sleep quality, and enhanced mental clarity. While anecdotal evidence supports these claims, more rigorous scientific research is needed to substantiate them fully.

In conclusion, emerging studies suggest that music tuned to 432 Hz may have therapeutic benefits, particularly in reducing anxiety and promoting relaxation. However, the existing research is limited, and further studies with larger sample sizes and diverse populations are necessary to confirm these effects and understand the underlying mechanisms.

Additional Evidence of the Validity of Sound Therapy

Due to the increased interest in sound therapy as a tool for promoting healing, many schools have started offering sound therapy certification courses. Below is a list of a few schools that offer a wide range of certification levels. In addition to on-site classes, many online opportunities are available, expanding access to a wider range of students.

1. **Globe Sound Healing Institute:**
   Located in Sausalito California, this school provides hands-on training with tuning forms, voice, crystal bowls, and sound technology. You can receive advanced practitioner training as well as an Associate Degree. Website: https://soundhealingcenter.com

2. **Sound Healing Academy:**
   This is a UK-based academy offering three levels of certification. It covers the instruments of tuning forks, gongs, singing bowls, voice and shamanic drums. Website: https://academyofsoundhealing.com

3. **The British Academy of Sound Therapy (BAST):**
   While also located in the UK, it does provide some online courses. Their programs include a diploma in "Group Sound Therapy Training" and "Sound Therapy Training," which focuses on one-to-one therapy. They provide a strong focus on research-based therapeutic methods. Website: https://britishacademyofsoundtherapy.com

4. **Sound Healing Training (Jonathan Goldman's School):**
   The founder, Jonathan Goldman, is a pioneer in modern sound healing. He offers online courses, workshops, and retreats focused on the science and spirituality of sound. Website: https://www.healingsounds.com

If you're drawn to a more structured route in pursuing a sound healing career path, exploring a degree in music therapy may be the perfect fit. Today, many universities offer bachelor's and master's programs in this field. Music therapy is a recognized clinical practice grounded in research that uses music to support healing on physical, emotional, cognitive, and social levels. Music therapists serve people of all ages and backgrounds in diverse environments such as hospitals, schools, rehab centers, hospices, mental health facilities, and private practices. Common practices include music listening, improvisation, singing, songwriting, guided music imagery, movement, instrument playing, and drumming.

The average cost for certification courses is outlined in the table below. This does not include the cost of a bachelor's or master's degree.

Overall Average Price Ranges

Program Type	Typical Price (USD)
Intro/Foundations Course	$250–$500
Practitioner Certificate	$1,500–$3,500
Advanced/Full Diploma	$2,500–$5,000+
Self-Paced Workshops	$100–$600

Chapter 3

INSTRUMENTS AND TOOLS
FOR SOUND HEALING

Music can change the world because it can change people.

—BONO

Tibetan Singing Bowls

SINGING BOWLS HAVE BEEN cherished for centuries, not just as musical instruments but as powerful forces in meditation and healing. Each bowl tells a story steeped in history and culture, ready to guide you on a sonic journey. Whether you're looking for peace, clarity, or a deep sense of connection, these bowls offer a gateway to a more balanced life.

The origins of singing bowls trace back to the rugged landscapes of the Himalayas, where Tibetan monks have long used them in their spiritual practices. Traditionally made from a unique alloy of metals like copper, silver, and gold, each bowl is handcrafted with its own distinctive sound. Tibetan singing bowls are not just instruments; they are vessels of spiritual energy. When struck or played with a mallet, they produce rich, harmonic tones that resonate deeply, inviting a meditative state. Surrounded by the soothing hum of metal and crystal tones, you can feel their vibrations wrap around you like a gentle embrace—purifying the space, calming your mind, and restoring inner balance.

Choosing your first singing bowl is an adventure in itself. Instead of picking the shiniest or the biggest one, find the bowl that speaks to you. Consider the material, as different metals produce different tones. Older bowls often have richer, warmer sounds, while newer ones provide a brighter, metallic tone. Size matters, too, as larger bowls tend to have deeper, more resonant sounds. Don't rush this process. Spend time exploring various bowls, striking them gently with a mallet to feel their vibrations. The right bowl will resonate with you on a personal level, creating a connection that feels just right.

Once you've found your bowl, the next step is learning how to play it. The goal isn't just to make sound; it's to create an experience. Start by holding the bowl in the palm of your hand or placing it on a cushion. Using a mallet, gently strike the bowl's rim to awaken its voice. To sustain the sound, run the mallet around the rim with a firm but gentle pressure, allowing the vibrations to build and fill the space.

Experiment with different striking techniques and pressure to discover the full range of tones your bowl can produce. This is an art, a dance between you and the bowl, where each movement brings forth a new layer of sound.

Integrating singing bowls into your sound healing practice can profoundly enhance your journey. These bowls are not just tools; they are companions in meditation, helping to quiet the mind and release tension. The soothing tones promote relaxation, reducing stress and anxiety.

When used in meditation, singing bowls can deepen focus, allowing you to explore your inner world with clarity. Each session with a singing bowl invites you to connect with your body's natural rhythms, aligning your energy and bringing balance to your life.

Exercise: Finding Your Bowl's Voice

Once you have chosen the bowl you want to use in your meditation, sit with your singing bowl for a few quiet moments. Close your eyes and gently strike the bowl. As the sound resonates, notice how it feels in your body. What emotions or sensations arise? Try running the mallet around the rim and listen to the changes in tone and vibration. Allow yourself to be present with the sound, exploring the relationship between you and your bowl. This practice involves not only playing the bowl but also listening deeply and connecting with its energy.

Tuning Forks: Precision Tools for Frequency Healing

Though unassuming in appearance, tuning forks are highly effective tools in sound healing. When struck, a tuning fork vibrates at a specific frequency, generating sound waves that travel through the air and deeply resonate within the body. This interaction with the body's energy field helps restore balance and promotes well-being.

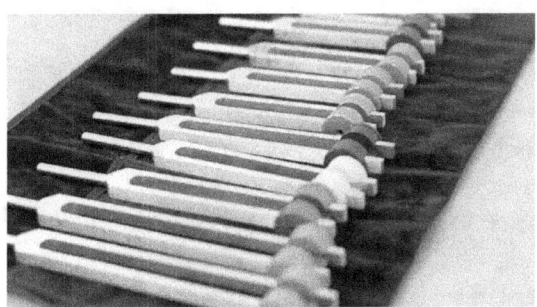

There are two main types you'll encounter: weighted and unweighted. Unweighted forks vibrate in the air and are great for clearing energy fields around you. In contrast, weighted forks have a small weight at the end, allowing them to be placed directly on the body for deeper vibration, making them ideal for physical healing.

These forks are often tuned to specific frequencies, like the 128 Hz fork, popular for its calming and grounding effects. Each frequency serves a different purpose, from promoting relaxation to stimulating energy flow.

Using tuning forks effectively in a healing session is an art that combines technique and intuition. You begin by activating the fork. Hold it by the stem and strike it gently against a rubber mallet or a soft surface. This action sets the fork vibrating, creating a pure tone you can use in your healing practice. If you're using a weighted fork, gently place the end on the body, targeting areas that need attention, such as a tense muscle or an energy center like a chakra. If you're working with an unweighted fork, you can move it around the body, allowing the vibrations to wash over you and balance your energy field. The key is to listen and feel, noticing how your body responds to the vibrations and adjusting your approach accordingly.

The therapeutic applications of tuning forks are diverse and impactful. They are often used for balancing energy fields and chakras, helping to align the body's energetic system. This alignment can lead to harmony and well-being by reducing stress and promoting relaxation. But tuning forks don't just influence energy; they have physical benefits, too.

With their ability to reduce pain and inflammation, tuning forks serve as a natural complement to other therapies. More than just a tool for relaxation, they help release physical tension, improve circulation, and ease muscle aches—offering a holistic path to well-being.

Choosing the correct set can feel overwhelming if you're new to tuning forks, but it doesn't have to be. Start by considering your budget and what you hope to achieve with sound healing. A basic set with a few key frequencies, like 128 Hz and 136.1 Hz, is a great start. These frequencies are versatile, offering benefits for both mind and body.

As you become more comfortable with tuning forks, you can expand your collection by adding specific frequencies tailored to your needs. Explore different types and see which ones resonate with you. Whether you're looking to ease stress, enhance meditation, or relieve physical discomfort, there's a tuning fork that can support your journey.

> **Reflection Section: Listening to Your Body**
> Take a moment to reflect on how your body responds to different sounds. Try using a tuning fork on various points of your body and notice the sensations it evokes. How does the vibration feel? Does it bring up any emotions or memories? Keep a journal of your experiences, noting any shifts in your energy or mood. This practice can deepen your connection to your body and enhance your understanding of sound healing.

The Healing Drum: Rhythms That Revitalize

A circle forms, each person holding a drum, eyes closed, as rhythmic beats fill the air. The sound creates an unspoken unity, resonating deep within. Across cultures, drumming has been a vital part of healing traditions, offering more than just rhythm—it serves as a gateway to spiritual and emotional connection.

The African djembe drum is a perfect example. More than an instrument, it's a storyteller and a bridge to ancestral wisdom. In many African communities, its rhythms play a key role in communal healing by fostering connection and continuity. Used in ceremonies, the drum's vibrations are believed to cleanse negative energy and restore balance to the soul.

In Native American cultures, drums are considered sacred and often used in ceremonies to connect with the spirit world. Each beat is a prayer, a heartbeat echoing the pulse of Mother Earth. These drums come in various sizes and are often adorned with intricate designs, each carrying spiritual significance.

During ceremonies, the rhythmic drumming helps participants enter a trance-like state, where they can connect with their inner selves and the world around them. It's a powerful tool for emotional release, allowing buried emotions to surface and be processed in a safe, supportive environment.

Rain drums and steel tongue drums, more modern additions to the drumming family, offer a soothing, melodic sound that is often used in personal meditation and relaxation practices. The soft, pattering sounds of rain drums mimic the gentle fall of rain, creating a calming atmosphere ideal for stress relief.

Steel tongue drums, on the other hand, provide a more melodic experience. Their tongues cut into the drum's surface to produce different notes. They're easy to play, making them accessible to those new to drumming, and their harmonious tones can help soothe the mind and body.

Drumming doesn't just produce sound; it creates an experience. When you drum, you're not just playing an instrument; you're engaging with a powerful form of therapy. The repetitive rhythms can induce altered states of consciousness, much like meditation. The drumbeat is a guide, leading you to a deeper understanding of yourself. This experience can promote emotional release, helping you process and let go of pent-up feelings. It's a physical and emotional form of expression that transforms the act of drumming into a dialogue between you and your soul.

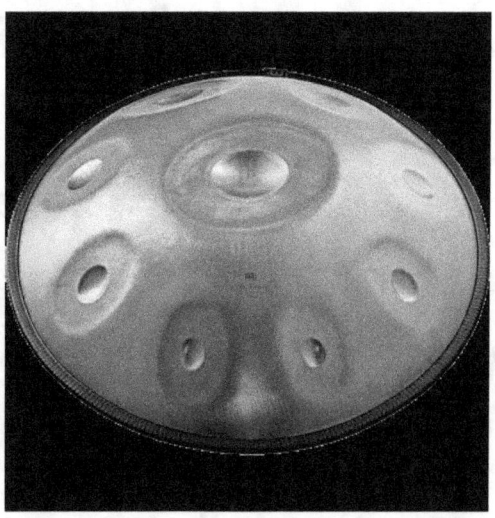

Selecting the right drum is a personal journey. Consider what you're drawn to. Is it the deep, resonant bass of a djembe or the calming melody of a steel tongue drum? Think about the drum's size and material. Larger drums offer a more powerful sound, while smaller ones are easier to handle and transport.

Once you have your drum, learning to play is the next step. Start with basic techniques, like striking the drumhead with your hands or using mallets for different tones. Practice simple rhythms, feeling the vibrations travel through your body. Allow yourself to explore, finding rhythms that resonate with your inner beat.

Drumming is a communal experience as much as it is a personal one. Drum circles are a fantastic way to connect with others through rhythm. In these gatherings, each participant contributes to the collective sound, creating a powerful sense of unity. Drum circles can be organized informally with friends or as part of community events.

They offer a space for shared healing, where the collective rhythm becomes a force for emotional and spiritual connection. These sessions can be deeply transformative, as the shared energy amplifies the healing power of the drums. Whether you're drumming alone or with others, let the rhythm guide you, offering a path to revitalization and peace.

Crystal Bowls: Harnessing the Power of Quartz

Crystal singing bowls bring a contemporary touch to ancient sound healing practices. Emerging in popularity in the late 20th century, these bowls are crafted from quartz crystal, producing clear, resonant tones. Each bowl is precisely tuned to align with specific chakras, the body's energy centers, helping to restore balance and harmony.

Whether you're looking to balance your heart chakra or awaken your third eye, there's a crystal bowl that resonates at the ideal frequency to assist you. The transparency of these bowls symbolizes clarity and enhances their healing properties, making them a favorite in sound baths and energy healing sessions.

Each bowl is tuned to a note corresponding to a chakra, from the root to the crown, making them ideal for balancing the body's energy system. The sound waves produced by playing a crystal bowl resonate with these energy centers, encouraging harmony and alignment throughout your body.

Choosing your crystal bowl is a deeply personal experience that involves finding a bowl that resonates with your energy. When selecting a bowl, consider its sound quality and resonance. Strike it gently and listen to the tones it produces. Does it feel soothing and harmonious? Pay attention to how its vibrations affect you. A good crystal bowl will produce a long, sustained tone with rich harmonics, creating a soundscape that invites relaxation and introspection.

Once you've found your perfect bowl, caring for it is simple. Clean it regularly with a soft cloth to remove dust and smudges, and store it in a safe place where it won't be knocked over or damaged.

Playing a crystal bowl requires a gentle touch and a mindful approach. To begin, place the bowl on a flat surface or hold it in your hand. Using a mallet, gently circle the bowl's rim, maintaining consistent pressure to create a sustained tone. The key is to move slowly and steadily, allowing the bowl's natural resonance to build over time.

You might notice harmonic overtones emerging as you play, adding depth and complexity to the sound. These overtones can be incredibly healing, creating a multi-layered soundscape that engages the mind and body. Experiment with different speeds and pressures to discover the range of sounds your bowl can produce. The experience is meditative and invigorating, offering a sense of peace and clarity that can enhance any healing practice.

Chapter 4

PRACTICAL TECHNIQUES FOR DAILY PRACTICE

Music produces a kind of pleasure which human nature cannot do without.

–CONFUCIUS

IT IS SO EASY to get caught up in the whirlwind of daily life, with stress building up like a pressure cooker. Embracing sound therapy is like having a magical pause button—a simple, quick reset that melts away tension in just minutes. This is where the beauty of sound healing comes in, offering you a moment of peace amidst the chaos. You don't need an extravagant setup or hours of spare time. Just a few mindful minutes can make a world of difference.

Let's explore some quick, sound healing exercises designed to fit snugly into your hectic schedule and provide a fast track to relaxation and balance. Start with a basic yet powerful technique: combining breathing exercises with a short sound session.

Find a comfortable spot, close your eyes, and take a deep breath. As you exhale, let out a gentle hum. Feel the vibrations resonate through your body, releasing tension with each breath. This simple exercise can be done anywhere, whether in a quiet corner of your home or while taking a breather at your desk. Pairing deep, rhythmic breathing with sound creates a calming effect that connects you to the present moment and eases the mind, much like a tranquil wave washing over your senses.

For those moments when you need a quick, targeted relaxation tool, try using a tuning fork. These nifty little instruments are perfect for on-the-spot stress relief. Strike the fork against a soft surface, like your palm, and gently place it on your temple or wrist. Feel the soothing vibrations spread, quieting your mind and relaxing your muscles. It's like having a gentle massage for your brain, providing instant calm wherever you are. Tuning forks are portable and easy to use, making them ideal companions for anyone needing a quick recharge during a busy day. Accessibility and convenience are key to incorporating sound healing into your daily routine.

Mobile apps with guided sound meditations are a fantastic resource, offering a variety of soundscapes at your fingertips. Whether on a lunch break or commuting, these apps provide a quick escape, guiding you through a calming journey with just the tap of a button. It's like having a pocket-sized sound bath you can access anytime, anywhere. These sessions are designed to fit your schedule, ensuring stress relief is just a click away.

Different environments require different techniques, and sound healing is adaptable to any situation. For example, you can use desk-based sound meditation with noise-canceling headphones at work. Choose a calming soundscape, like gentle ocean waves or a soft piano melody, and let it play softly in the background. This creates a peaceful bubble amidst office noise, helping you maintain focus and manage stress.

If you're on the go, try quick tonal humming. Creating sound can reset your mind, grounding you in the present and providing a quick burst of relaxation.

Stressors may still appear, but with sound healing, you're better equipped to handle them with grace. This practice encourages mindfulness, inviting you to pause and breathe, even in the busiest moments.

Interactive Element: Quick Sound Healing Techniques Checklist

- **Breathing + humming:** Find a quiet spot, breathe deeply, and hum on the exhale. Repeat for 2–3 minutes.

- **Tuning fork relaxation:** Strike the fork, place it on your temple or palm, and feel the vibrations for instant calm.

- **Mobile sound meditation:** Use a guided app during breaks for a quick escape. Try ocean waves or soft melodies.

- **Desk-based meditation:** Use noise-canceling headphones and play calming sounds at work for focus.

- **Tonal humming on the go:** Hum gently when stressed to reset your mind.

Regular practice turns these simple exercises into powerful tools for navigating life's challenges.

Creating a Sound Sanctuary: Setting Up Your Healing Space

Creating a sound haven doesn't require a lot of space or expense, just a bit of intention and creativity. Start by choosing a quiet, distraction-free area in your home. This could be a cozy corner in your living room or a spare room that doesn't see much use. The key is finding a spot that feels separate from the hustle and bustle of daily life.

Once you've selected your space, think about adding elements from nature. Plants are excellent for this; they improve air quality and bring a sense of peace and vitality. Consider adding a few succulents or a lush fern to your sanctuary. Crystals can also enhance the atmosphere, adding a touch of Earth's natural beauty.

The acoustics of your sanctuary play a crucial role in how sound resonates and affects you. To optimize sound quality, consider using soft furnishings. A plush rug, some throw pillows, or a couple of blankets can absorb excess sound, preventing harsh echoes and creating a warm, enveloping soundscape.

Arrange your sound healing instruments—whether singing bowls, tuning forks, or chimes—within easy reach. This ensures that everything is right at your fingertips when you feel the urge to play. The flow of sound in your space should feel natural, guiding you effortlessly into a state of relaxation.

Consider incorporating additional elements that enrich the sensory experience to elevate your sound sanctuary. Aromatherapy with essential oils can be a delightful addition. A few drops of lavender or eucalyptus in a diffuser can transform the atmosphere, calming the mind and invigorating the senses. Lighting also plays a vital role. Soft, ambient lighting, like that from a salt lamp or a few well-placed candles, can set a calming mood. The gentle glow creates a cozy ambiance that invites you to let go and relax. These elements work together to form a holistic healing environment where every sense is catered to, and every worry is left at the door.

Personalizing your sanctuary is where the magic truly happens. This is your space, so let it reflect who you are. You may have a favorite piece of art that inspires you or a family heirloom that brings comfort. Incorporate these into your space. They carry meanings and memories that resonate personally, enhancing the healing experience.

You might also consider setting up a small altar with items that hold significance for you—a shell from a cherished beach visit, a feather found on a peaceful walk, or a small statue representing tranquility. These personal touches transform a simple space into a sacred retreat. In this place, you can connect with yourself on a deeper level.

A sound sanctuary is a space that feels like an extension of yourself, a refuge where you can engage in sound healing practices freely and fully. You must look beyond the physical setup and focus on cultivating an environment that nurtures your spirit and encourages relaxation. As you fine-tune your space, allow it to evolve with you. Let it be a living, breathing part of your sound healing journey, adapting to your needs and reflecting your growth.

Sound Bath Rituals: Immersive Healing Practices

The essence of a sound bath is a deeply immersive experience that uses sound to promote full-body relaxation and emotional release. The beauty of sound baths is that they create a space where you can let go, allowing the sound to guide you into a state of profound relaxation. As the vibrations flow through you, they harmonize your mind and body, helping you find balance and inner peace.

During a sound bath, it's common to experience heightened awareness and emotional release. The sounds can bring buried feelings to the surface, offering a safe space to process and let go. This combination of relaxation and emotional exploration makes sound baths such a powerful tool for healing.

You don't need an elaborate setup to create your own sound bath at home. Start by selecting a few instruments that resonate with you. Singing bowls, gongs, and chimes are popular, each offering unique tones and vibrations. Arrange these instruments in a way that feels inviting. Consider layering the sounds to create a rich, immersive experience.

Begin with a soft, continuous tone, like the gentle hum of a singing bowl, and gradually introduce other sounds. Allow each layer to build upon the last, creating a rich soundscape that envelops you in tranquility. It's like painting with sound, where each note adds color and depth to the canvas of your experience. As you play, pay attention to how the sounds interact with each other and your body, adjusting as needed to maintain a harmonious flow.

Setting an intention for your sound bath can enhance the healing experience. Before you begin, take a moment to reflect on what you hope to achieve. You may be seeking relaxation, clarity, or emotional release. Whatever it is, hold that intention in your mind as you start the session.

Some people find it helpful to create a personal mantra or affirmation to focus their thoughts. You might say, "I am open to healing," or "I release what no longer serves me." This simple act of mindfulness can guide your experience, helping you stay present and connected to the sound. As the session progresses, return to your intention, letting it anchor you in the moment.

While personal sound baths are deeply rewarding, there's something special about experiencing sound healing in a group setting. Group sound baths offer a unique opportunity for community building, where shared vibrations amplify the healing potential. In a group, the collective energy enhances the experience, creating a sense of connection and support.

Group sessions provide a chance to come together with others, each person bringing their own intentions and experiences to the mix. Whether it's a community event or a small gathering with friends, group sound baths encourage you to explore sound healing in a new light. As you lie back, surrounded by others, the shared soundscape creates a powerful sense of unity, deepening your connection to yourself and those around you.

Morning Sound Rituals: Starting Your Day With Harmony

Morning routines have a way of setting the tone for the entire day, don't they? Imagine waking up to the gentle sound of an uplifting playlist, each note coaxing you from sleep into a state of alertness and positivity. This doesn't just involve hitting play on your favorite tunes; it requires mindfully choosing sounds that energize and inspire you.

A well-curated morning playlist can awaken your senses like a refreshing breeze on a warm day. It's a gentle yet powerful way to boost your mood and prepare your mind for whatever lies ahead. The right mix of melodies can make the difference between dragging yourself out of bed and stepping into your day with a spring in your step.

Now, let's talk about the power of your own voice. Short chanting or vocal toning exercises in the morning can stimulate energy flow and set a positive intention for the day. You don't need to be a trained singer to benefit from this. Find a comfortable place, take a deep breath, and let out a sound that feels right. Maybe it's a soft "om" or a simple hum.

The vibrations resonate through your body, waking up your mind and spirit. This practice encourages you to connect with yourself before the day's demands take over. It also enhances focus and sharpens mental clarity, preparing you for whatever challenges come your way.

The benefits of these morning sound rituals extend beyond immediate energy boosts. They play a crucial role in enhancing your overall well-being. By starting your day with sound, you're crafting a foundation of mental resilience and emotional balance. The soothing effects of sound can help buffer you against stress, making it easier to face the day's ups and downs with grace. You'll find that your mood lifts more easily, your patience extends further, and your mind stays clearer. Think of it as a morning elixir that nourishes your mind and soul, fortifying you from within.

Although mornings can be hectic, incorporating quick sound practices doesn't have to add to the frenzy. A five-minute sound meditation with tuning forks or chimes can be a game changer. Strike the fork or chime and let it resonate as you focus on your breath. This brief moment of mindfulness can ground you, creating a ripple effect of calm that carries through the day.

Alternatively, consider a sound walk. As you step outside, tune in to the sounds of nature. The rustle of leaves, birdsong, or even distant traffic can become a symphony that grounds and centers you. This connection to the natural world adds a layer of serenity to your morning routine.

Consistency is the secret ingredient to making these rituals work for you. While it's important to find what resonates, adapting these practices to suit your needs is equally vital. What works one morning might not work the next, and that's okay.

Start your week with an upbeat playlist to boost your energy and get ready for the week ahead, then wind down on Fridays with gentle chants to welcome the weekend. The idea is to develop a morning ritual that feels natural and enjoyable—something that enhances your routine rather than adds to your to-do list.

Personalizing your sound rituals ensures they serve you best, offering a unique blend of peace and energy tailored to your life.

Evening Sound Practices: Unwinding and Preparing for Rest

As the sun sets and the day winds down, it's time to shift our focus toward relaxation and prepare for a restful night. Evening sound practices offer a gentle transition from the hustle and bustle of daily activities to the calm embrace of sleep.

One effective way to ease into the evening is by playing calming music or nature sounds. Imagine letting the soothing melody of a gentle piano or the soft rustle of leaves carry away the day's stress. These sounds are a balm for your frazzled nerves, encouraging your body to relax and your mind to slow down. This simple ritual can transform your evening routine into a peaceful prelude to sleep.

Another wonderful way to mark the end of the day is by using a singing bowl. The resonant tone of a singing bowl can signal to your body and mind that it's time to unwind. As you gently strike the bowl, listen to the sound as it fills the room and resonates within you. This practice helps you let go of the day's worries and sets a calming tone for the night ahead. The vibrations from the bowl can help slow down your heart rate and deepen your breathing to prepare you for a good night's rest.

Consider incorporating guided sound meditation into your evening routine for deep relaxation. These meditations use sound to help quiet your mind and relax your body, making it easier to fall asleep. As you listen to the guided meditation, focus on the sounds and let them guide you into deep relaxation.

Another powerful tool for easing into sleep is binaural beats. Listening to these beats can help synchronize your brainwaves and promote relaxation, helping you enter a state of deep, restful sleep. These practices work together to create an environment that nurtures rest and rejuvenation.

A consistent evening routine is essential for enhancing sleep quality and overall well-being. By winding down with sound each evening, you signal to your body that it's time to relax and prepare for rest. This consistency helps train your body to recognize when it's time to sleep, helping you fall asleep more quickly and enjoy uninterrupted sleep throughout the night. Think of it as a gentle nudge for your body's internal clock, encouraging it to align with the natural rhythms of day and night. Over time, this routine can improve sleep quality, helping you wake up feeling refreshed and ready for a new day.

As we transition to the next chapter, remember that sound healing is a versatile tool that can support you in various aspects of life. Whether seeking relaxation, balance, or deeper self-awareness, sound offers a path to greater well-being. The journey continues with more practices and techniques that can transform everyday moments into opportunities for healing and growth.

Chapter 5

PERSONAL GROWTH AND INNER PEACE THROUGH SOUND

*Music has healing power. It has the ability to
take people out of themselves for a few hours.*

–ELTON JOHN

PICTURE YOURSELF SITTING IN a serene space, the hum of a single note enveloping you like a gentle embrace. This is sound meditation—a practice as ancient as it is transformative. While the world buzzes with activity, sound meditation offers a sanctuary where time seems to slow, allowing you to connect with a deeper part of yourself.

You've likely heard of meditation as a tool for mindfulness, but adding sound to the mix creates a unique experience. The resonance of a single note or the melody of an instrument can ground you and anchor your wandering mind. As you focus on the sound, you cultivate a nonjudgmental awareness, letting thoughts drift by like clouds in the sky.

Integrating sound into meditation shouldn't complicate the practice but enhance it. Guided sound meditations with ambient soundscapes can transport you to peaceful realms, where stress and tension become distant memories. Imagine the gentle rustle of leaves or the soft chime of a bell guiding your breath, each sound inviting you to go deeper. Chanting mantras or using vocal toning can also deepen your focus.

The vibrations produced by your voice have a unique way of aligning your thoughts, bringing clarity and calmness. It's like tuning an instrument; every note brings you closer to harmony.

Sound meditation offers a multitude of benefits, especially for mental clarity. Engaging with repetitive sound patterns can reduce mental chatter and create space for new insights to emerge. In addition to finding peace in the moment, you enhance your cognitive function and emotional regulation.

Studies show that sound therapy can significantly reduce tension, anxiety, and depression while boosting spiritual well-being. When one's mind is clearer, one can approach challenges with a fresh perspective and make decisions with confidence and ease.

Creating a personal sound meditation practice is an adventure in self-discovery. Begin by experimenting with different sound sources, like bells, chimes, or even a soothing playlist of binaural beats. Let your curiosity guide you as you explore various sounds and their effects on your mind and body. Notice which sounds resonate with you, bringing a sense of peace or energy. Over time, you'll find a routine that feels natural and fulfilling.

Consistency is key, so try to incorporate sound meditation into your daily life. Whether it's a few minutes in the morning or a longer session before bed, these moments can become a cherished part of your routine.

Interactive Element: Creating Your Sound Meditation Routine

- **Explore different sounds:** Spend a week trying out different instruments or playlists. Notice which ones bring you the most peace and clarity.

- **Set a regular time:** Choose a specific time each day for your practice. Consistency helps establish a habit.

- **Reflect on your experience:** Keep a journal of your sound meditation experiences. Note any changes in mood, focus, or stress levels.

- **Adjust as needed:** As your practice evolves, tweak your routine to better suit your needs and preferences.

By embracing sound as a tool for mindfulness, you're opening the door to personal growth and inner peace. This practice encourages presence, not perfection. It's about finding those moments of stillness where you can reconnect with yourself, guided by the gentle whisper of sound.

Whether you're new to meditation or a seasoned practitioner, sound meditation offers a fresh and enriching perspective, inviting you to explore the depths of your mind with curiosity and kindness.

Exploring the Inner Self: Sound as a Tool for Introspection

Sound can be a powerful mirror, reflecting the emotional states that often lie beneath the surface. It's like opening a door to parts of yourself that you might not always acknowledge. Have you ever noticed how certain songs can bring up feelings you weren't even aware you had?

Sound acts as a bridge to deeper layers of consciousness, encouraging introspection that reaches beyond everyday thoughts into your soul, allowing you to explore hidden emotions and thoughts with gentle curiosity. By engaging with sound, you can tap into these deeper layers, where self-discovery and personal growth await.

To use sound for introspection, try creating a ritual that includes journaling with sound prompts. Begin by choosing a sound that resonates with you—maybe it's the soft strumming of a guitar or the soothing hum of a Tibetan bowl. Close your eyes and focus on the sound, allowing it to guide your thoughts. As you listen, let your mind drift and explore whatever comes up.

Afterward, jot down your reflections. What emotions surfaced? Did any memories or insights appear? This practice can uncover insights you might not find through traditional journaling alone. It's a way to let sound lead you into self-discovery, revealing parts of yourself that might have been tucked away.

Another technique is sound-induced visualization. This involves allowing sounds to inspire mental images, offering a pathway to the subconscious. Find a quiet spot, choose a calming soundscape or instrumental piece, and close your eyes. Let the sounds paint pictures in your mind. Imagine walking through a serene forest or floating on a gentle sea. These images can help you explore your inner world, providing clarity and understanding.

Visualization with sound is a relaxing, non-threatening way to access buried emotions and thoughts. By engaging with these images, you can begin to understand and release emotional blockages that might be holding you back.

The transformative potential of sound-based introspection lies in its ability to foster personal growth and self-awareness. By regularly engaging in these practices, you can begin to identify patterns or emotional triggers that influence your behavior.

Sound offers a safe space to explore these areas, encouraging you to release negative emotions you've held on to. Imagine sound as a gentle companion, helping you peel back the layers of your psyche to reveal your true self. This introspection can lead to profound changes, shifting your perspective and opening you to new possibilities. This journey of self-discovery can enhance your understanding of who you are and what you need.

Approach sound-based introspection with an open and compassionate mindset. Set intentions for your sessions, focusing on what you hope to learn or release. You may want to understand a recurring emotion or find peace with a past experience. Whatever your goal, approach it with kindness, allowing yourself to explore without judgment. This is your space to grow and heal; there's no right or wrong way to engage with it.

As you work with sound, remember to let your intuition guide you in this process, leading you to insights and understanding. Each session is an opportunity to connect with yourself on a deeper level, embrace your complexities, and celebrate your growth.

Sound Healing for Emotional Balance: Techniques to Soothe the Soul

Sound has a unique way of reaching the depths of our emotions, pulling out what words sometimes can't express. Different sounds trigger different feelings, and this is where sound healing steps in as a powerful tool for emotional balance.

Specific frequencies, like the gentle hum of Tibetan bowls or the warm tones of a guitar, have a calming effect on our emotional states. They can soothe anxiety, ease stress, and even help regulate our moods. It gently balances the soul, using vibrations to shift emotional patterns and promote inner peace.

One practical approach to using sound for emotional balance is sound journaling. This involves consciously listening to specific sounds and noting how they affect your emotions. Certain music calms your mind, while other sounds energize you. By tracking these responses, you gain insights into what sounds resonate with you emotionally. For instance, a soft piano piece might help you process sadness, while the upbeat rhythm of a drum could lift you out of a funk.

This practice helps you understand your emotional triggers and equips you with a toolkit of sounds to manage them. Think of it as a personalized emotional first aid kit, ready to soothe the soul whenever needed.

Playing specific music or sounds can also counteract negative emotions. Imagine you've had a tough day. The stress is palpable, and your mind is racing. Playing a calming soundscape or your favorite relaxing tunes can act as a balm, easing the tension and helping you find your center. Instead of distracting yourself, you are using sound to create a positive emotional shift.

The right music can guide you through emotional turmoil, allowing you to process feelings in a healthy way. Over time, you'll notice that these sound interventions can transform how you handle stress, boosting your resilience and emotional stability.

Regular sound healing practice offers lasting benefits for emotional health. By incorporating it into your routine, you cultivate a sense of balance that extends beyond the moment. Consistent exposure to healing sounds can improve your ability to handle stress and emotional upheaval, making you more resilient in the face of life's challenges.

You become like a tree with deep roots, swaying gently in the storm but never breaking. Over time, this resilience becomes part of your natural response, allowing you to navigate emotional highs and lows with grace and confidence.

Choosing the right sounds for emotional healing is a personal journey that involves exploring different sound sources to find what resonates with your unique emotional landscape. Start by experimenting with various sounds, from classical music to nature soundscapes, and observe how each makes you feel. You might discover that the sound of rain brings you comfort or that a particular melody helps you focus.

Create a personalized playlist of these sounds, a go-to resource for emotional support. This playlist becomes your companion, offering solace and strength whenever needed.

As you engage with sound healing for emotional balance, remember that the focus is on self-exploration and discovery. There's no right or wrong way to experience sound; it's just what feels right for you. Allow yourself to be guided by your intuition and the wisdom of your emotions. Sound invites you to listen deeply, to connect with your inner world, and to find harmony amidst the chaos.

Journeying Within: Soundscapes for Inner Peace

Soundscapes are audio environments crafted to evoke deep relaxation and inner peace. They immerse you in layers of natural sounds, offering an escape from the noise and stress of daily life. It feels like stepping into a private sanctuary, where the world slows down, and tranquility takes center stage. The immersive experience of soundscapes allows your mind and body to unwind, creating a peaceful refuge from external stressors.

Crafting your own personalized soundscape can be a rewarding and creative venture. Start by thinking about the natural sounds that bring you comfort and ease—perhaps the soft patter of rain on a roof, the gentle roll of ocean waves, or the melodic call of birds at dawn. These sounds can be combined with instrumental music, like the soothing notes of a flute or the gentle strum of a guitar, to enhance the calming effect.

Layering these elements creates a rich soundscape that envelops you in peace, each layer adding depth and texture to your personal oasis. Creating these soundscapes invites you to explore different combinations, discovering what resonates most with your spirit.

The psychological benefits of soundscape immersion go beyond mere relaxation. They offer a mental escape, a chance to reset and recharge. By providing a break from the constant barrage of modern life, soundscapes help reduce anxiety and foster a sense of peace. It's like taking a mini-vacation without leaving your home, allowing your mind to wander and explore new landscapes.

Research shows that engaging with nature sounds can significantly reduce stress and improve overall well-being. This connection to nature, even through sound, has a profound calming effect, promoting mental clarity and emotional balance.

Feel free to experiment with different soundscape elements to enhance your inner peace. Incorporate environmental sounds that speak to your soul, whether it's the rhythmic crash of waves or the soft chirping of crickets at dusk. Depending on your preference, these sounds can be mixed with ambient music or left to stand alone. The beauty of soundscapes lies in their versatility; they can be tailored to fit any mood or moment. Certain sounds might work better in the morning to energize you, while others are perfect for winding down in the evening. Exploring these elements opens you to a world of self-discovery, where you learn what truly soothes and nurtures your spirit.

Interactive Element: Crafting Your Personal Soundscape

- **Collect your favorite sounds:** Gather recordings of natural sounds and music that resonate with you. This could be anything from rain falling to ocean waves or even cityscapes

- **Layer and experiment:** Use audio editing software or apps to layer these sounds, experimenting with different combinations and volumes. Don't be afraid to play around until you find the perfect mix.

- **Create different versions:** Consider making different soundscapes for various times of the day or emotional states. One might be more energizing, while another is calming.

- **Listen and reflect:** Spend a few minutes daily immersed in your soundscape. Notice how it affects your mood and stress levels. Adjust as needed to enhance your experience.

Soundscapes offer a personal and immersive way to find peace. As you explore and create, let your intuition guide you, revealing the sounds and combinations that bring you the greatest sense of tranquility and joy.

Manifesting Intentions: Using Sound for Personal Empowerment

What could you achieve if you woke up each day with a clear vision of your goals, feeling empowered and ready to tackle whatever comes your way? The power of sound can play a significant role in turning these intentions into reality. By vocalizing intentions with affirmations and sound, you can amplify the energy behind your personal goals.

Picture starting your day by speaking your desires aloud, accompanied by the gentle hum of a tuning fork or the soothing tone of a singing bowl. As you voice your intentions, the sound resonates within you, reinforcing your commitment and aligning your energy with your goals. It's like setting a powerful vibration in motion, echoing your desires into the universe.

Consider incorporating specific frequencies that align with your intention's energy to harness sound in empowerment practices. Certain frequencies resonate with different aspects of life, such as creativity, abundance, or healing. Using these frequencies, you can fine-tune your focus and enhance your resolve. Chanting or toning can also strengthen your determination, offering a rhythmic mantra that grounds your intentions in reality. Each chant becomes a step forward, a declaration of your commitment to personal growth. Using sound in this way boosts your confidence and helps clear away self-doubt, allowing your true potential to shine through.

Sound plays a powerful role in fostering a positive mindset and boosting confidence and motivation. When you incorporate sound into your intention-setting practices, you are giving yourself an auditory pep talk that motivates you to push forward and overcome obstacles.

You can create an environment that supports your aspirations by choosing sounds that inspire and uplift you. Whether it's the drum's uplifting beat or the flute's inspiring notes, these sounds can help shift your mindset, turning challenges into opportunities and doubts into determination.

Integrating sound into daily intention rituals can be a transformative experience. Consider designing a daily sound ritual that affirms your goals and intentions. This could be as simple as starting your morning with a few minutes of focused sound meditation, where you visualize your intentions while surrounded by sound.

Or you could end your day by reflecting on your progress, using sound to celebrate your achievements and reaffirm your commitments. The key is to make sound an integral part of your routine, allowing it to support and reinforce your journey toward your goals. Over time, these small, consistent practices can lead to significant shifts, empowering you to live with purpose and intention.

As we wrap up this exploration of sound and personal empowerment, consider how you can incorporate these practices into your daily life. By embracing sound as a powerful tool for personal growth, you craft an environment where your intentions can thrive. Each tone and vibration becomes a stepping stone on the path to realizing your dreams, offering a constant source of strength and encouragement. With sound as your guide, you have the tools to manifest your desires and create a life that resonates with your true self. As we move forward, let's continue exploring how sound can enhance our physical and emotional well-being. The journey is just beginning, with the next chapter offering new insights and techniques to deepen your practice.

Make a Difference With Your Review

Unlock the Power of Generosity

The best way to find yourself is to lose yourself in the service of others.

–MAHATMA GANDHI

Helping others brings a sense of joy that's hard to match. Would you join me in spreading that joy?

Imagine someone, just like you, looking for simple, practical ways to manage stress, rebuild resilience, and feel more at peace. Your review could be the guiding light they need to begin their journey.

My goal with *Body Wisdom Through Sound Therapy* is to make the tools for healing and connection easy and accessible for everyone. But to reach more people, I need your help. When someone chooses a book, they often rely on reviews. A few kind words from you could:

- help someone take their first step toward healing.

- encourage another person to rebuild their resilience.

- inspire someone to reconnect with their body and inner peace.

- bring more light into someone's life.

It costs nothing, takes just a moment, but could change everything for someone searching for hope.

How to leave a review:

Simply scan the QR code or visit the link below to share your thoughts.

http://amazon.com/Body-Wisdom-Through-Sound-Therapy-eboo
k/dp/B0F6GPJQH9

If this book has helped you in any way, I'd love to hear about it—and so would others.

Thank you for being a part of this journey. Your generosity means the world to me.

Warmly,
Grace Bailey

Chapter 6

OVERCOMING SKEPTICISM AND BUILDING CREDIBILITY

Music acts like a magic key, to which the most tightly closed heart opens.

—MARIA VON TRAPP

YOU ARE AT A family gathering when someone unexpectedly asks about your new interest in sound healing. You start explaining the calming effects of a singing bowl, only to be met with raised eyebrows and a skeptical chuckle. Has that ever happened to you?

It's not uncommon to encounter skepticism when discussing alternative therapies like sound healing. Yet, the truth is that sound healing is more than just a whimsical trend. It's backed by science and has a growing place in modern wellness. Let's dive into some myths surrounding sound healing and set the record straight.

One of the most persistent myths is that sound healing is merely a placebo. Some folks claim the benefits are all in your head. But here's the kicker: Sound healing has been clinically shown to influence physiological health factors.

A study published by the National Library of Medicine highlights that sound therapy can improve mental states like anxiety and depression, even aiding in cancer treatment. In addition to boosting mood, it creates tangible changes in how our bodies and minds function.

Sound interacts with our physiology through vibrations, affecting everything from cell growth to stress regulation. It's far from a placebo; it's a scientifically supported treatment option with real, measurable benefits.

Another common misconception is that sound healing is purely spiritual—a mystical practice with no basis in reality. While it's true that sound healing has deep roots in spiritual traditions, it's also firmly grounded in science. The therapeutic effects of sound, such as those observed in Tibetan singing bowl meditation, have been documented to significantly reduce tension, anxiety, and depression while boosting spiritual well-being.

This intersection of science and spirituality highlights sound healing's applicability in contemporary wellness. It's about finding a balance where evidence-based practices meet personal experience.

In today's world, sound healing is no longer confined to niche wellness circles or esoteric retreats. It's entering mainstream health practices and gaining traction in mental health treatments, offering a noninvasive, calming complement to traditional approaches.

Imagine walking into a therapy session where, instead of just talking, you also experience the soothing vibrations of sound. This integration is proving effective, as sound therapy helps lower stress levels, enhances mood, and supports mental clarity. In stress management programs, sound healing is used to help individuals unwind, providing a natural way to cope with life's pressures.

Cultural stereotypes often cloud perceptions of sound healing. Some people wrongly associate it with cultural appropriation or dismiss it as an exotic curiosity. It's crucial to distinguish between cultural appropriation and respectful practice. Sound healing draws from diverse traditions, each with its own rich history and significance. Respectful practice involves acknowledging these origins and understanding the cultural context. By honoring the source cultures and practicing mindfulness, we can appreciate the depth and diversity that sound healing brings to our lives.

The holistic benefits of sound healing are undeniable. Beyond relaxation, it provides a comprehensive approach to well-being. By considering both scientific evidence and experiential insights, we can appreciate sound healing's multifaceted nature. It addresses the mind, body, and spirit, offering a path to enhanced health and happiness.

Interactive Element: Myth–Busting Checklist
- **Myth 1:** Sound healing is just a placebo.

  - **Reality:** It is clinically proven to improve mental states and physiological health.

- **Myth 2:** Sound healing is purely spiritual.

  - **Reality:** It is grounded in science with documented therapeutic effects.

- **Myth 3:** Sound healing is cultural appropriation.

  - **Reality:** Respectful practice honors and acknowledges cultural origins.

As we continue to explore sound healing's potential, it's clear that this practice is more than just a passing trend. It's a valuable tool in our wellness arsenal that invites us to listen, feel, and heal.

Evidence-Based Sound Healing: Studies That Support Its Efficacy

Sound healing might involve "feel-good" vibes, but there's also a solid stack of research backing its effectiveness. Let's start with anxiety and depression. Studies have shown that sound healing can significantly reduce symptoms of these mental health issues.

One study observed participants taking part in sound therapy sessions, many of whom started off with feelings of stress, anxiety, and depression. The results revealed a clear reduction in anxiety and a boost in mood. This isn't just coincidence—it's the science of sound waves influencing our mental state.

The vibrations and frequencies work their magic, helping to calm the mind and soothe the soul. When you listen to a singing bowl or tuning fork, the pleasant sound also transmits a wave of energy that can help balance your emotional state.

Pain is another area where sound healing shows promise. Chronic pain can be relentless, impacting every aspect of life. Yet, sound therapy offers a noninvasive way to manage it. Studies have found that sound vibrations interact with our nervous system, potentially reducing our pain perception.

Imagine the relief of finding a tool that can ease pain without the side effects of medication. Sound healing offers that possibility, helping people find peace in their bodies.

The methodologies behind these studies lend them credibility. Researchers don't just gather people and hope for the best. They carefully design studies with control groups and, in some cases, double-blind testing. This means that neither the participants nor the researchers know who's receiving the sound therapy, which helps eliminate bias.

Studies that follow participants over extended periods help uncover the long-term benefits of sound healing. This comprehensive approach ensures that the results provide reliable insights into sound's healing potential.

These studies offer practitioners a treasure trove of information. Knowing that sound healing is backed by science boosts confidence in the practice. It also helps build trust with clients who might be skeptical about trying something new.

When you can point to research showing real benefits, it makes it easier to incorporate sound healing into clinical settings. Imagine a therapy session where sound healing enhances traditional techniques, offering clients a holistic approach to wellness.

If you're curious and want to dive deeper, a whole world of research awaits you. Journals specializing in complementary and alternative medicine are great places to start. They publish studies that explore the effects of sound healing and other holistic practices.

A quick web search on integrative health will reveal a wealth of many sources of information.

Databases like PubMed offer access to a wide range of articles, giving you the chance to explore the science behind sound therapy. It's like having a library of knowledge at your fingertips, ready to expand your understanding and appreciation of sound healing.

How to Discuss Sound Healing With Skeptics

We've all been there—trying to explain why sound healing isn't just some quirky hobby but a legitimate path to wellness, only to be met with skepticism. Dealing with skeptics requires a mix of tact, patience, and strategic communication.

Start by embracing the power of active listening. When someone questions your interest in sound healing, genuinely listen to their concerns. Are they worried it's not scientific enough? Or do they think it's just a fad? By understanding their perspective, you can respond in a way that addresses their doubts. Pair this with empathy. Show them you understand where they're coming from. Validate their concerns before sharing your own insights. This approach can turn a confrontation into a conversation.

Framing sound healing within a scientific context can be a game changer. Instead of leaning solely on personal beliefs, link your explanations to scientific studies and evidence. Mention how sound therapy has been shown to lower anxiety and manage pain. People often find it easier to accept something when science backs it up.

When discussing the benefits, sprinkle in terms like "vibrational frequencies" or "nervous system regulation." These phrases highlight the physiological effects without sounding too technical. By grounding the discussion in science, you can bridge the gap between skepticism and curiosity.

Sharing personal experiences can be another powerful tool. Sometimes, a real-life story resonates more than any data point. Talk about your own journey with sound healing. Maybe you found peace during a chaotic time or experienced unexpected relief from chronic pain. Describe the sounds that moved you and the changes you noticed. Personal anecdotes have a way of bypassing logical barriers and tapping into emotional understanding.

When people see how sound healing has impacted your life, they're more likely to consider its potential benefits for themselves.

Education is another key player in overcoming skepticism. Encourage skeptics to explore sound healing further on their own. Suggest peer-reviewed articles or reputable resources where they can read up on the topic.

The National Center for Complementary and Integrative Health is a great place to start. It offers credible information on alternative therapies, providing a balanced view that might shift people's perspectives. Knowledge is empowering, and when people learn more, they often become more open-minded. Sharing resources shows you're not just pushing an agenda but genuinely interested in informed discussions.

Patience and openness go a long way in these conversations. Remember, not everyone will be convinced, and that's okay. It's important to recognize when to agree to disagree. Keep the conversation respectful, and try not to take skepticism personally. Everyone's on their own path, and sometimes, it takes a while for new ideas to sink in. You create a space where curiosity can flourish by remaining open and engaging without judgment. Even if a skeptic doesn't walk away ready to try sound healing, they might leave with a little more respect for your views.

Ultimately, discussing sound healing with skeptics isn't about winning an argument. The goal is to gently plant seeds of curiosity and understanding. By combining empathy, science, storytelling, and patience, you can engage in meaningful dialogues that open minds and hearts.

Recognizing Reliable Sources: Navigating Information Online

Navigating the ocean of information online can feel daunting. There's so much out there, and not all is trustworthy. When searching for information on sound healing or any health-related topic, knowing how to sift through the noise and find credible sources is crucial.

First, take a look at who wrote the content. Check the author's credentials and affiliations. Are they experts in their field? Do they have relevant experience or education? This can give you a good idea of whether the information is reliable. Additionally, cross-reference their claims with reputable publications. If well-known journals or respected health organizations publish their findings, it's more likely that the information is accurate.

It's easy to fall into the trap of clickbait and sensationalist headlines, especially when they promise quick fixes or miraculous results. These catchy titles are designed to grab your attention but often don't deliver on their promises. Instead, they lead to articles that care more about generating clicks than providing quality content. Be wary of headlines that sound too good to be true and always read with a critical eye.

Bias is another pitfall to watch out for. Some articles might have a hidden agenda, promoting specific products or viewpoints. It's important to read between the lines and ask yourself if the information is presented objectively.

Knowing where to turn is helpful when you're looking for trustworthy content. Academic databases like PubMed are goldmines of peer-reviewed studies and articles. These resources offer a wealth of reliable information backed by research and scientific rigor. They're great for diving deep into specific topics and understanding the evidence behind sound healing.

In addition to academic databases, plenty of trustworthy wellness websites and journals are available. Look for sites that are transparent about their sources and regularly updated. Organizations like the National Center for Complementary and Integrative Health, mentioned earlier, provide balanced and evidence-based information on alternative therapies, including sound healing.

Critical thinking is your best friend when evaluating online information. Don't take everything you read at face value. Question the claims being made and consider whether they're supported by evidence. If a source makes bold assertions without backing them up, it's worth doing a little digging to verify the information.

Engage with content analytically, and don't be afraid to challenge what you're reading. This approach helps you build a more nuanced understanding of sound healing and its benefits. It promotes being an informed consumer who makes decisions based on solid evidence rather than hype.

Reflection Section: Evaluating Online Sources

Next time you read an article or blog post on sound healing, take a few minutes to evaluate its credibility. Ask yourself: Who wrote this, and what are their qualifications? Do reputable sources back the claims? Does the article seem unbiased, or is it pushing a particular agenda? By taking these steps, you'll be better equipped to discern quality information from the noise, empowering yourself with accurate and valuable knowledge.

Building Your Confidence: Trusting Your Personal Experience

Nothing compares to the personal insights you gain along the way as you explore sound healing. Trusting your own experience is an empowering and vital part of your healing process. Each session with sound is a chapter in your story, revealing new layers of understanding and growth. As you explore the world of vibrations and frequencies, you notice changes—perhaps you're sleeping better, feeling calmer, or finding clarity in moments of chaos. These shifts, though they may seem small, are significant markers of your progress. They're reminders that your journey with sound is unique, and the insights you gain are invaluable.

One of the most effective ways to track these changes is through self-assessment. Consider keeping a sound healing journal—a dedicated space to document your experiences, reflections, and observations. Each entry is a snapshot of your progress, capturing the nuances of your journey. Write about the sounds that resonate with you, the emotions they stir, and the physical sensations they invoke.

Over time, you'll accumulate insights that track your growth and serve as a source of inspiration. This practice of reflection helps you recognize patterns, appreciate your progress, and build confidence in your path.

Self-reflection exercises can further deepen your understanding of sound healing's impact on your emotional and mental well-being. Take a moment after each session to sit quietly and assess any shifts in your mood or mindset. Ask yourself questions like, "How do I feel compared to before the session?" or "What emotions came up, and why?" This introspective practice forges a deeper connection with your healing journey, allowing you to trust the process and your own intuition. It encourages tuning in to the subtle changes that occur, acknowledging them, and embracing them as part of your growth.

Engaging with sound healing communities can also be incredibly beneficial. Sharing experiences with others on a similar path provides support, encouragement, and fresh perspectives. Whether joining an online forum or attending local group sessions, being part of a community enriches your experience. It's a space to discuss challenges, celebrate milestones, and learn from others' insights. The feedback and encouragement you receive can bolster your confidence, reinforcing that you're on the right track. Plus, the sense of belonging and shared purpose can be a powerful motivator.

Continuous learning and adaptation are key to maintaining a vibrant and effective sound healing practice. The world of sound is vast and ever-evolving, with new techniques and insights constantly emerging. Stay curious and open-minded and be willing to explore new methods and tools. Attend workshops and training sessions to expand your knowledge and refine your skills. Each experience adds depth to your practice, enhancing your understanding and confidence. Embrace the opportunity to grow, knowing that every bit of knowledge you gain enriches your healing journey.

As you continue to explore the possibilities of sound healing, remember that your personal experience is a rich blend of insights, growth, and transformation. Trust in the process, and allow your own journey to guide you. In the next chapter, we'll explore how to integrate sound healing into daily life, making it a seamless part of your routine.

Chapter 7

Integrating Sound Healing Into a Busy Lifestyle

*The vibrations of sound can directly influence the rhythms of our bodies,
restoring balance and harmony.*

—Unknown

Life often feels like a nonstop race. With work, family, and personal commitments pulling you in different directions, finding a peaceful moment can seem nearly impossible. But what if there was a way to seamlessly incorporate sound healing into your daily routine without adding extra stress?

What if you could pause, breathe, and reset in just a few moments, no matter where you are? Sound healing provides this opportunity—a brief escape from the chaos, allowing you to recharge without rearranging your entire day. Let's explore how you can effortlessly integrate sound healing into your routine on even the busiest of days.

Time-Saving Techniques: Sound Healing on the Go

For many of us, fitting sound healing into our already packed schedules can feel daunting. But here's the good news: It doesn't have to be time-consuming. Consider starting with short breathing exercises paired with a tuning fork or a small bell. These tools are compact and easy to carry, making them perfect for a quick reset.

Find a quiet corner, close your eyes, and strike the tuning fork. Let its gentle vibration guide your breath, inhaling deeply and exhaling slowly. Even a few minutes can help center your mind, reducing stress and boosting focus.

Making sound healing a part of your daily routine is easier than you think. A quick five-minute sound meditation during your lunch break can help reset your mind. Simply find a quiet place, put on your headphones, and tune into calming soundscapes. Resources like iAwake Technologies, Insight Timer, and Wholetones offer a wealth of audio tracks designed to promote relaxation and mindfulness, making it effortless to integrate into your day.

Whether you're sitting at your desk, taking a short walk, or lying in bed before you start your day, these meditations can be a lifesaver. They offer a mental pause that recharges your energy for the rest of the day.

Consider integrating sound healing into other routine, everyday activities. For instance, why not use a meditation app with sound features during your daily commute? These apps transform your journey into a calming experience, turning traffic jams and crowded trains into opportunities for relaxation.

The iAwake Technologies app, for example, provides a vast selection of soundscapes and meditations that cater to different needs, from stress relief to enhanced concentration. It's a digital oasis at your fingertips, ready to transport you into a serene state of mind whenever needed.

The cumulative benefits of these brief, regular sound sessions are substantial. Even short practices, when done consistently, can significantly improve your overall well-being.

Imagine experiencing reduced stress levels and increased mental clarity simply by incorporating a few mindful moments into your day. The key is consistency—making sound healing a regular habit, even if it's just for a few minutes each day. Over time, these small actions add up, helping you build resilience against stress and enhancing your ability to focus and be present.

Interactive Element: Quick Sound Healing Checklist

- **Morning boost:** Start your day with a brisk walk while listening to a five-minute sound meditation.

- **Midday reset:** Use a tuning fork or bell during your lunch break to realign your energy.

- **Commute calm:** Transform your daily commute to work with a soothing soundscape on your favorite meditation app.

- **Evening unwind:** End your day with a short sound bath before bed.

The beauty of sound healing lies in its adaptability. It fits effortlessly into even the busiest of lifestyles. Whether you're stuck in traffic, waiting in line, or taking a moment to breathe, there's always room for a touch of sound healing magic.

Sound Healing for the Workplace: Techniques for Stressful Environments

Sometimes, work environments can feel like pressure cookers. Looming deadlines, nonstop meetings, and endless emails can leave you tense and frazzled. But what if you could find moments of calm amidst the chaos? Sound healing offers a discreet and effective way to bring tranquility to your workday.

One simple method is using noise-canceling headphones. They don't just block distractions; they become your personal sanctuary. Slip them on during a break and indulge in a few minutes of sound meditation. The soothing tones can transport you to a calm place, even at your desk. The vibrations of calming music or nature sounds can help reset your mind, leaving you refreshed and ready to tackle the next task with renewed focus.

For those who prefer a more tactile approach, consider keeping a small, personal sound device at your desk. This could be a portable speaker or even a mini singing bowl. When stress levels rise, a quick sound session can work wonders. Just a minute spent listening to or creating gentle sound waves can shift your mood and reduce anxiety.

These devices help you practice sound healing effortlessly, without drawing attention or interrupting your workspace. They offer a quiet, personal remedy for stress, always within reach.

Integrating sound healing into work breaks can make a big difference in how you feel throughout the day. Quick sound breaks are like hitting a mental refresh button. They provide a moment to breathe, helping you escape the pressure and regain clarity. This boosts your mood and productivity. You're more focused and efficient when your mind is clear and relaxed. Imagine stepping away from your desk, closing your eyes, and letting the sound wash over you. It's a simple yet powerful way to recharge, ensuring you return to work with a sharper mind and a calmer spirit.

Creating a calming work environment can also enhance your well-being. Ambient soundscapes can reduce the noise that often fills an office. Low-volume nature sounds or soft instrumental music can create a soothing backdrop, promoting peace even in a bustling workspace.

This harmonious environment benefits you and can uplift your colleagues, fostering a more serene and productive atmosphere. It transforms your workspace from a source of stress into a haven of tranquility.

Sound healing can also play a surprising role in team-building and group wellness. Consider organizing group sound meditation sessions. These collective experiences can strengthen coworkers' bonds and enhance the workplace culture. Imagine gathering with your team for a short guided meditation session where everyone can relax and unwind.

These sessions promote relaxation, camaraderie, and unity, making wellness a shared priority. Such practices can improve communication, collaboration, and morale, creating a workplace where everyone feels supported and valued.

So, whether seeking personal tranquility or aiming to enhance your team's well-being, sound healing offers a versatile solution. It's a gentle reminder that even in the busiest environments, you can always find room for peace.

Balancing Sound Practices With Technology: Apps and Tools

In today's fast-paced, tech-driven world, integrating sound healing into your life has never been easier, thanks to a plethora of digital tools and apps. These resources make sound healing accessible and customizable to fit your unique lifestyle.

Sound Therapy apps like iAwake Technologies, Insight Timer, and Calm provide an extensive library of soundscapes, guided meditations, and breathing techniques. With over 150,000 tracks on Insight Timer alone, you can find the perfect session to match your mood. Whether you need a moment of calm before bed or a mindful start to your day, these apps make sound therapy effortless. Their versatility turns them into a pocket-sized wellness space, ready whenever you are.

Beyond apps, there are also devices designed to generate healing frequencies. These gadgets can range from small, portable sound machines to more sophisticated tools like frequency generators that you can set to specific healing tones. The convenience of these devices is their ability to bring the transformative power of sound to any space, be it your living room or office.

Imagine turning your home into a sanctuary of sound, where every corner hums with vibrations that promote relaxation and wellness. These technologies bridge the gap between traditional sound healing practices and modern living, allowing you to incorporate healing frequencies into your environment easily.

Technology offers numerous advantages in sound healing. It enhances accessibility, allowing you to engage with sound therapy without needing specialized equipment or extensive knowledge. Digital tools offer customizable sound settings, letting you adjust frequency, volume, and type of sound to suit your preferences. This personalization means you can tailor each session to address specific needs, whether seeking stress relief, improved focus, or a deeper meditative state. Moreover, the convenience factor is undeniable—having these resources at your fingertips means you can easily fit sound healing into your daily routine and lifestyle.

Selecting the right technology for sound healing involves some exploration. When choosing apps, consider the user interface and ease of use. An intuitive design can make a difference, especially when using the app for relaxation. Opt for apps that offer various sound options, from nature sounds to binaural beats, so you have plenty of options to explore.

When choosing a device, prioritize ease of use and range of frequencies. The goal is to find tools that enhance your experience without adding complexity. Remember, the best technology is the one that aligns with your personal preferences and lifestyle.

While technology offers incredible benefits, it's important to use it mindfully. It's easy to get lost in the digital world, so setting limits on screen time is crucial to maintaining focus on the healing experience. Consider using technology as an enhancement to, rather than a replacement for, traditional sound healing practices. For instance, you might use a meditation app to guide your practice but still appreciate the tactile experience of playing a singing bowl or a tuning fork. Balancing digital and traditional practices ensures that you remain present and engaged with the healing process, allowing you to fully experience the benefits of sound therapy.

Creating a Portable Sound Healing Kit

The beauty of a portable sound healing kit is that you can carry a mini sanctuary of peace with you wherever you go, transforming any space into a calming oasis. Let's start with the essentials. A set of miniature tuning forks or chimes can be incredibly effective. They're small, easy to use, and designed to produce soothing frequencies that instantly shift your mood. Picture yourself on a lunch break, feeling the weight of the day press down on you; then, with just a gentle strike of a tuning fork, you're back to feeling grounded and centered.

Next, consider adding a small, lightweight singing bowl to your kit. These bowls are perfect for quick relaxation sessions. Their resonant tones can fill a room with calming energy, ideal for those moments when you need a mental escape. Whether in a hotel room or a quiet corner of a park, a few minutes with a singing bowl can bring you back to a state of balance by creating a little pocket of peace. A travel pouch is essential for keeping everything organized, protected, and accessible when needed. Picture a neatly packed pouch tucked into your bag, its contents a secret weapon against stress.

Customization is key to making your sound healing kit truly yours. Consider including personal affirmations or intention cards. These small additions can enhance your practice, focus your mind, and reinforce your goals. Whether a card with a simple mantra or a note that reminds you of your intentions, these personal touches can deepen your connection to the practice.

Your kit may include a small crystal or a photo that holds special meaning, further personalizing your experience. The goal is to create a kit that resonates with you, reflecting your unique journey and supporting your well-being.

The importance of portability cannot be overstated. In our fast-paced world, easy access to your sound healing tools encourages frequent use. When everything you need is compact and ready to go, you're more likely to incorporate sound healing into your daily life.

Imagine reaching into your bag and finding precisely what you need to calm your mind or lift your spirits. Sound healing should be a natural, effortless part of your routine. With your portable kit, you can seize those little moments throughout the day, creating opportunities for relaxation and renewal whenever you need them.

Sound Healing for Travelers: Maintaining Your Practice on the Road

A portable sound healing kit is a game-changer, ensuring you can maintain your practice no matter where life takes you. Travel often brings chaos and unpredictability, but with your kit, you can find balance even in the most unfamiliar settings. In the middle of a noisy airport, the soothing vibrations of your singing bowl can transform the space into a personal retreat and help maintain a sense of calm.

Fortunately, sound healing can be your travel companion, helping to ease anxiety and promote relaxation during these times. Portable sound devices, like small speakers or even sound apps on your phone, can transform any hotel room into a sanctuary. Place a speaker on the nightstand, play soothing soundscapes, and let the gentle sound waves create a peaceful atmosphere, helping you unwind after a long day of travel.

During flights or layovers, sound meditation can provide a peaceful escape from the chaos. With eyes closed and headphones on, a meditation app leads you into a state of relaxation, while the steady hum of the plane becomes a soothing backdrop to your moment of tranquility.

This practice helps pass the time and reduces flight anxiety and jet lag. It feels like bringing a piece of home with you, keeping you grounded as you soar through the skies. For those long stretches of waiting, these moments of sound meditation can transform the airport lounge into a place of serenity, offering a break from the chaos around you.

The benefits of sound healing go beyond relaxation; they provide relief from the stresses of travel. Long trips can be draining, but sound therapy helps ease anxiety, soothe nerves, and restore balance. By making sound healing a part of your travel routine, you arrive at your destination feeling refreshed and ready to embrace new experiences. This gentle yet effective tool ensures that each journey is as enjoyable as the destination itself.

Exploring local sound healing practices can add a rich layer to your travels. Different cultures have unique approaches to sound healing, and immersing yourself in these practices can be both enlightening and enriching. Attend local workshops or events to experience traditional sound healing methods firsthand. Whether a sound bath in a Japanese temple or a drum circle in an African village, these experiences offer a deeper connection to the places you visit. They provide a unique perspective that allows you to engage with the culture more profoundly. Every place has its own sonic signature that enhances your understanding and appreciation of the world around you.

Integrating sound healing into your travel itinerary can be as simple as scheduling short sound sessions during downtime. Consider setting aside a few moments each day to engage in sound healing, whether during your morning routine or as you wind down in the evening. These sessions don't need to be lengthy; even a few minutes can make a significant difference. They offer a chance to reconnect with yourself amidst the excitement of travel, grounding you and helping maintain your sense of well-being. By making sound healing a part of your travel routine, you create a touchstone—a familiar practice that offers comfort and stability no matter where you are.

As we wrap up this chapter, remember that the essence of this sound healing is flexibility and adaptability. Whether you're on the road or busy at home, sound healing is a versatile tool that fits into any lifestyle, offering peace and balance wherever life takes you. In the next chapter, we'll explore how sound healing can build community and connection.

Chapter 8

COMMUNITY AND CONNECTION

Rhythm and harmony find their way into the inward places of the soul.

—PLATO

HAVE YOU EVER FOUND yourself in a room full of strangers and felt an unexpected sense of belonging? It's like joining a conversation where, even in moments of silence, everything makes sense. This is the magic of community, especially when it involves sound healing.

As you explore this practice, you'll discover that it's not just about the sound itself but the connections you forge along the way. Being part of a sound healing community can elevate your practice to new heights, offering you a space to learn, share, and grow with others who share your passion.

Finding Your Tribe: Joining Sound Healing Communities

One of the most powerful aspects of joining a sound healing community is the shared learning and support from like-minded individuals. Attending a local sound healing workshop brings together people with a shared goal: exploring the transformative power of sound. You could find yourself next to someone with years of experience, eager to share their wisdom, or sitting beside a newcomer just as excited to learn and grow alongside you.

This diversity of experience creates a strong network of knowledge, where each person contributes their unique perspective. It gives you access to a living library filled with stories, tips, and insights you can draw upon at any time.

Finding these communities can be as simple as a quick online search. Look for local meetups or clubs that focus on sound healing. These gatherings are often advertised on community boards, wellness centers, or social media platforms. Joining online forums or social media groups dedicated to sound healing can also be a great way to connect with others.

These virtual spaces offer a treasure trove of resources, from instructional videos to lively discussions about techniques and experiences. Whether you prefer face-to-face interactions or the comfort of a digital community, there's a place for you to connect and grow.

The beauty of sound healing communities lies in their diversity and inclusivity. Engaging with diverse voices and experiences enriches your understanding of sound healing. Each culture brings its unique approach to the practice, offering new techniques and perspectives to explore.

For instance, you might learn about the intricate rhythms of African drumming or the calming chants of Tibetan monks. Respecting and incorporating these cultural approaches into your practice can deepen your appreciation for the art of sound healing. It opens your mind and heart to the world of possibilities different cultures bring.

Active participation is key to getting the most out of your community experience. Share your personal insights and experiences with others. You might have a unique approach to playing your singing bowls or a story about how sound healing helped you through a tough time. Sharing these experiences enriches the community and strengthens your own practice. Consider volunteering at community events or gatherings—for example, helping set up a local sound bath or organizing an online discussion group. These contributions help build a supportive, thriving community where everyone feels valued and inspired. Your involvement makes a difference.

Interactive Element: Community Connection Checklist

- **Research local groups:** Check community centers, wellness boards, and online platforms for sound healing meetups.

- **Engage online:** Join social media groups and forums focused on sound healing to connect with a broader audience.

- **Value diversity:** Attend events or watch videos that explore sound healing from different cultural perspectives.

- **Share your voice:** Contribute your experiences and insights through storytelling or teaching others.

- **Volunteer:** Offer your time and skills at events to strengthen community bonds and learn more.

By actively seeking out and engaging with sound healing communities, you open yourself to a world of learning and support. These connections can transform your practice, providing knowledge and a sense of belonging. As you immerse yourself in the collective energy of a sound healing community, you'll find that the journey becomes more meaningful and enjoyable.

Hosting Sound Healing Circles: Creating Shared Experiences

Creating and hosting a sound healing circle might initially seem daunting, but it can be incredibly rewarding. Start by choosing a suitable venue. Look for a quiet and comfortable space with good acoustics. This could be a cozy room in your home, a community center, or even an outdoor garden if the weather permits.

Once your location is set, think about the flow of the session. Structure is important, so plan activities that guide participants through different phases of sound healing. You might begin with a grounding exercise, like deep breathing or gentle stretching, to help everyone settle into the space. Then, progress into the main sound session, starting with soft chimes or bells and gradually building to more resonant instruments like singing bowls or gongs. Aim to create a journey through sound that touches on various emotions and energies, leading participants to a place of calm and introspection.

Facilitating an inclusive and welcoming environment ensures everyone feels comfortable and engaged. Encourage participants to share their thoughts and feelings during and after the session. Open dialogue fosters trust and connection, allowing individuals to feel seen and heard. It's also helpful to establish guidelines for respectful participation—for example, being mindful of noise levels, honoring each person's space, and maintaining an open, nonjudgmental attitude. Setting these expectations creates a safe space where everyone can explore sound healing without fear of judgment or interruption.

To keep the sessions engaging and impactful, consider incorporating a variety of instruments and sound practices. You might introduce instruments that participants are less familiar with, such as rain sticks or handpans, to add new layers of sound. Or, use theme-based sessions to focus on specific intentions or outcomes. For instance, a session centered on gratitude might include sounds that evoke warmth and comfort, encouraging participants to reflect on what they are thankful for.

Alternatively, a session to release stress could feature instruments that produce soothing, calming tones, helping participants release tension. These variations keep the sessions fresh and allow participants to explore different aspects of their sound healing journey.

It's important to remember that each sound healing circle is a chance to create a unique shared experience. The group's collective energy amplifies the practice's effects, fostering connections that can lead to deeper healing and personal growth. As participants share their insights and experiences, they contribute to a supportive community where everyone is a teacher and a learner.

These gatherings offer more than a shared practice; they amplify the collective energy, turning each session into a powerful shared healing experience. When you sit in a circle, surrounded by others who are open to the healing potential of sound, you feel a deeper bond that words alone can't describe. It's as if the collective heartbeat of the group pulses through each note and vibration, creating an environment where healing can flourish.

Hosting a sound healing circle is an opportunity to unite people and create a space where sound can use its magic to transform the ordinary into the extraordinary.

Online Sound Healing: Leveraging Digital Platforms for Connection

In the age of technology, sound healing has carved out a thriving niche online, opening doors to vast digital landscapes where sound knows no boundaries. These platforms bring together practitioners and learners from every corner of the globe, creating a network of shared experiences and knowledge that was once unimaginable.

With this modern technology, you can sit in your living room while a sound healer in Bali teaches you techniques that have been refined over centuries. The accessibility and reach of online platforms mean you can dive into this world from anywhere. The internet has made it possible to expand your practice and connect with others who share your passion, breaking down geographical barriers and creating a global community of sound enthusiasts.

The strategic use of digital platforms can significantly enhance your sound healing journey. Start by exploring online webinars and virtual sound baths. These sessions often feature experienced practitioners who share their expertise and guide you through immersive experiences.

Participating in these events broadens your knowledge and allows you to explore different styles and techniques. Interactive workshops and live sessions offer another layer of engagement, where you can ask questions, exchange ideas, and receive immediate feedback. These real-time interactions create a sense of connection and continuity, making online learning feel personal and engaging.

Creating a safe and supportive online space is essential for building positive digital environments. This involves setting clear community guidelines that promote respectful interaction. Encourage an atmosphere where everyone feels comfortable sharing their thoughts and experiences without fear of judgment by ensuring that discussions remain constructive and diverse perspectives are valued. Establishing these guidelines helps cultivate a space where participants feel respected and valued, allowing learning to flourish. The goal is to create a digital sanctuary where individuals can explore sound healing in a harmonious and supportive environment.

The wealth of resources available online is staggering, from online courses and tutorials to digital sound libraries. These resources provide a flexible way to learn at your own pace, allowing you to revisit concepts as needed. Whether you're a beginner looking to understand the basics or an experienced practitioner seeking advanced techniques, the internet is a treasure trove of information waiting to be explored. These resources can significantly enhance your practice, offering new insights and inspiration.

Digital technology gives you access to a vast library of sounds, musical instruments, and guided meditations, all readily available at your fingertips. These resources can enhance your understanding and refine your skills, making your sound healing practice more fulfilling and effective.

Interactive Element: Digital Engagement Checklist

- **Explore webinars:** Search for upcoming sound healing webinars to expand your knowledge.

- **Join virtual sound baths:** Participate in online sound baths to experience diverse practices.

- **Engage in live workshops:** Look for interactive workshops where you can ask questions and connect with others.

- **Set guidelines:** Ensure any online community you join has clear guidelines promoting respectful interaction.

- **Utilize online resources:** Access digital sound libraries and tutorials to enhance your learning.

The beauty of online sound healing communities is the diversity they offer. By engaging with learners and practitioners worldwide, you gain exposure to a wide array of practices and philosophies. This diversity enriches your understanding and broadens your perspective, allowing you to see sound healing through multiple lenses. You might discover a new technique that resonates with you or learn about a cultural practice that deepens your appreciation for the art of sound. Online platforms offer a unique opportunity to explore and experiment, helping you find your path in the world of sound healing.

Sound Healing Events: Attending Workshops and Retreats

In-person workshops and retreats offer immersive experiences that can deepen your understanding and practice of sound healing like nothing else. These events bring together expert practitioners who share their wisdom and techniques, providing you with enlightening hands-on learning opportunities. You get to experiment with different instruments, explore new methods, and engage with others who share your passion, all within a nurturing environment designed to support your personal growth.

When considering which workshop or retreat to attend, it's important to evaluate the credentials and approach of the facilitators. Look for those with a track record of experience and expertise in sound healing. Reading reviews from past participants can provide valuable insights into what you can expect. Additionally, consider the location, duration, and cost of the event. Some retreats are tucked away in remote areas, offering a complete escape from the hustle and bustle of daily life, while others might be closer to home, making them more accessible. Think about how much time you can commit and what fits within your budget. A weekend retreat might offer a quick recharge, while a week-long immersion can provide a more in-depth exploration.

The potential for personal transformation at these events is immense. Being fully immersed in sound healing allows for focused practice and reflection that helps you uncover deeper layers of yourself. You might experience shifts in your perceptions, release old patterns, or find new clarity about your life's path. The concentrated time spent in a retreat setting often leads to major breakthroughs. It's like pressing the reset button on your life, giving you the space to realign with your inner self and intentions. As you engage with the practices and teachings, you find yourself more open, receptive, and ready to embrace change and growth.

After attending a workshop or retreat, integrating new skills and insights into your daily practice is crucial. Keeping a journal of your experiences and takeaways can be incredibly beneficial. Write down what you learned, how you felt, and any realizations you had. This reflection helps solidify your learning and provides a reference for the future. Sharing your insights with local or online communities can also be valuable. Discussing your experiences with others reinforces your understanding and contributes to the community's collective knowledge. By sharing, you inspire and encourage others on their sound healing paths.

These events are more than an escape; they are a stepping stone to a deeper, more connected practice. As you leave the retreat or workshop, you carry with you memories and a toolbox of skills and insights to enhance your life. The techniques you learn can become a part of your daily routine, helping you maintain the peace and balance you experienced.

Whether incorporating a new meditation practice or using a specific instrument, these elements become integral to your sound healing journey. The community you build during these events can continue to support you long after you've returned home, providing encouragement and shared experiences as you explore the world of sound healing.

In the next chapter, we will explore how to make sound healing financially accessible, ensuring that this transformative practice can be a part of anyone's life.

Chapter 9

FINANCIALLY ACCESSIBLE
SOUND HEALING

*Music is the language of the spirit. It opens the secret of life,
bringing peace, abolishing strife.*

–KAHLIL GIBRAN

WHAT IF I TOLD you that you reap the benefits of sound healing without breaking the bank? When you embrace the Do It Yourself (DIY) process, you can tailor your tools to your personal preferences while saving money. In this chapter, we'll explore how you can use everyday items to create your own sound-healing instruments that infuse your practice with a personal touch.

Creating your own sound healing instruments is a journey of discovery. You can start with something as simple as a metal bowl from your kitchen; with creativity and the proper technique, it becomes a makeshift singing bowl. You can coax beautiful, resonant tones that soothe the mind and body by gently striking or rubbing its rim with a wooden spoon. It's amazing how an ordinary object can be transformed into a tool for relaxation and meditation. Not only does this approach make sound healing more accessible, but it also adds a layer of personalization to your practice. Each bowl will have its unique sound, reflecting the materials and methods you used to bring it to life.

If you're feeling crafty, try making a simple drum using recycled materials. Start by finding an empty coffee can or a large plastic container. Cover the open end with a piece of sturdy fabric or an old bicycle tire inner tube, securing it tightly with a rubber band or string. You've just created a drum with a rich, deep tone that is perfect for grounding and centering. Drumming can be a powerful way to connect with the rhythm of life, and the process of making your own drum can be incredibly rewarding. Plus, you're giving new life to materials that might otherwise end up in the trash.

For those looking to bring the sound of rain indoors without the wet mess, consider crafting a rain stick. These instruments mimic the soothing sound of falling rain and are surprisingly easy to make. You'll need a cardboard tube—like the kind from a paper towel roll—some small beads or rice, and a few toothpicks. Poke the toothpicks through the tube at various angles, then fill the tube with your beads or rice. Seal the ends, and voila! You've got a rain stick that brings a little piece of nature into your home. Rolling it gently can create a calming soundscape, perfect for meditation or relaxation.

Crafting a simple shaker can add a playful element to your sound healing practice. You only need a small container, like a plastic egg or film canister, and rice or dried beans. Fill the container, seal it up, and have a shaker that can add rhythm and texture to your sound sessions. Experiment with different fillings to achieve varied sound effects—for example, beans produce a heavier, more pronounced shake, while rice offers a softer, more subtle sound. This tinkering encourages mindfulness and creativity, reminding you that sound healing is as much about the journey as it is about the destination.

Creating your own instruments is both practical and therapeutic. This creative process can enhance your mindfulness and deepen your connection to the practice. As you decorate your instruments, perhaps painting them with colors or symbols that resonate with you, you're infusing them with your energy and intention. This personalization makes your instruments more than just tools; they become an extension of your healing journey. The satisfaction of using something you've made with your own hands in your sound healing practice is unparalleled. It empowers you, enriches your experience, and makes each session uniquely yours.

DIY Sound Instrument Crafting Guide

1. **Metal Bowl Singing Bowl:**

   - **Materials:** metal bowl, wooden spoon

   - **Instructions:** Gently strike or rub the rim with the spoon to create sound.

2. **Recycled Material Drum:**

   - **Materials:** coffee can/plastic container, fabric/tire inner tube

   - **Instructions:** Cover the open end, secure it tightly, and enjoy the deep tone.

3. **Rain Stick:**

   - **Materials:** cardboard tube, rice/beads, toothpicks

   - **Instructions:** Insert toothpicks, fill with rice/beads, seal, and roll to mimic rain.

4. **Simple Shaker:**

- **Materials:** small container, rice/beans

- **Instructions:** Fill, seal, and shake to add rhythm to your practice.

So, gather your supplies, clear some space, and let your creativity flow. Your sound healing instrument is waiting to be crafted, ready to bring tranquility and joy into your life.

Affordable Alternatives: Cost-Effective Instruments and Resources

Exploring the world of sound healing doesn't mean you have to empty your wallet. If you're just starting out or looking to expand your collection without breaking the bank, plenty of budget-friendly options are available.

For example, plastic or ceramic singing bowls offer a great alternative to traditional metal ones. While they may not have the same historical allure, they produce beautiful tones that can still create a soothing atmosphere. These materials are more affordable, lighter, and easier to handle, making them perfect for beginners. You can find these bowls online or at local markets, where you might even have the chance to try them out before buying.

Bamboo flutes are another fantastic option for those seeking simple melodic sounds without the hefty price tag. With their soft, soothing tones, bamboo flutes make a beautiful and calming addition to any sound healing practice. They're easy to play, making them accessible for anyone, even those with no musical background. Plus, their natural material resonates beautifully, creating calming vibrations that can enhance your meditation or relaxation sessions. You might find bamboo flutes at music stores, craft fairs, or even online, often at a fraction of the cost of more elaborate instruments.

Purchasing second-hand instruments is a smart way to acquire quality tools at a lower cost. Thrift stores, online marketplaces, and garage sales can be treasure troves for sound healing enthusiasts. You never know if you might find a vintage piece with a story to tell. When shopping second-hand, it's crucial to assess the instrument's condition. Check for any visible damage or signs of wear that might affect its sound quality. Play it, if possible, to ensure it produces the desired tones. A well-maintained second-hand instrument can offer just as much beauty and functionality as a new one, often with the added charm of a storied past.

Evaluating the quality of affordable sound healing instruments requires discernment. When you're out shopping, focus on sound quality and structural integrity. For example, when looking at singing bowls, listen for a clear, sustained tone. A good bowl should resonate deeply and consistently without any harsh or jarring overtones. For flutes, ensure that the instrument is free of cracks and all notes play smoothly. If you're unsure what to look for, consider bringing along a friend with more experience or seek advice from online sound healing communities. Remember, a higher price doesn't always mean better quality. Sometimes, the best finds are the ones that simply resonate with you, both in sound and spirit.

In today's digital age, innovative, low-cost resources are just a click away. Smartphone apps can simulate the sounds of various sound-healing instruments, including tuning forks. These apps allow you to explore different frequencies and techniques without needing to purchase multiple physical instruments. They can be a great way to experiment and find what resonates with you before making a financial commitment.

Additionally, free digital libraries offer a vast array of nature sounds that can be incorporated into your practice. The gentle rustle of leaves, the soothing flow of a stream, or the distant call of a loon can all enhance your sound healing sessions. These resources provide a rich soundscape that can complement your instruments by adding depth and complexity.

Expanding your sound healing practice doesn't have to be an expensive endeavor. With a bit of creativity and resourcefulness, you can find affordable alternatives that serve your needs beautifully. Whether it's through second-hand treasures, budget-friendly instruments, or digital resources, the key is to explore and experiment with what works best for you. Sound healing is a deeply personal journey, and the tools you choose should reflect your unique preferences and needs. So go ahead, explore the possibilities, and let the sounds guide you to a place of tranquility and balance.

Free and Low-Cost Sound Healing Resources

The world of sound healing is at your fingertips, offering a plethora of free resources that can transform your practice without costing a dime. Platforms like YouTube offer guided sound meditation videos ranging from ten-minute sessions to hour-long immersions, each designed to guide you into a state of relaxation and mindfulness. These resources are perfect for those who are just dipping their toes into sound healing or for anyone looking to expand their practice without a financial commitment. I have often enjoyed the Malte Martin Method channel on YouTube. (https://www.youtube.com/watch?v=mSqciTAlH7Q). He uses handpans to create beautiful, relaxing music.

Beyond the digital realm, your local community could be a goldmine of free sound healing opportunities. Many community libraries have collections of sound healing books and CDs, allowing you to explore different techniques and philosophies at no cost. It's a wonderful way to dive into the world of sound healing literature and discover new insights and practices. Some libraries even host workshops or talks on sound healing, providing a space to learn and connect with others who share your interests. When you tap into these local resources, you enrich your sound healing journey.

Similarly, community centers are often hubs for free classes and events, and sound healing is no exception. You might find free courses or sound baths organized in your area, offering a chance to experience sound's collective energy and healing power in a group setting. These events can be incredibly powerful, as the shared experience amplifies the healing effects. Public parks sometimes host free sound baths, where you can lie under the open sky and let the natural environment enhance the healing experience. It offers a beautiful opportunity to connect with nature and community while enjoying sound's therapeutic benefits.

Online, the abundance of free digital content is astounding. Podcasts dedicated to sound healing techniques are plentiful, offering everything from expert interviews to guided sessions. These podcasts allow you to learn on the go, whether you're commuting, exercising, or just relaxing at home. They provide insights into different practices and philosophies, often featuring experts who share their knowledge and experiences. The variety of podcasts lets you explore a wide range of topics, tailoring your practice to your specific needs and interests.

While free resources offer a wealth of opportunities, don't overlook the value of free trials for premium sound healing content. Many meditation apps, like Calm or Headspace, offer trial periods that let you explore premium features without the initial investment. These apps often have extensive libraries of soundscapes, meditations, and courses designed to deepen your practice. A trial period can be a great way to assess whether these premium resources align with your needs and goals. It gives you a sneak peek into a world of expanded possibilities, helping you decide if you're ready to commit.

The beauty of these free and low-cost resources is their accessibility and variety. They allow you to explore, experiment, and expand your understanding of sound healing without financial pressure. Whether you're drawn to digital content, local events, or trial offers, there's something for everyone. The key is to stay curious and open-minded, letting these resources guide you as you explore the many facets of sound healing. With so much available at no cost, you're free to dive into this practice, discovering what resonates most with you and enriching your life with the healing power of sound.

Maximizing Value: Investing Wisely in Your Sound Healing Journey

When stepping into the world of sound healing, it's easy to get swept up in the allure of all the instruments and resources available. But, let's face it, our budgets don't always match our enthusiasm. The key is to invest wisely, making sure each purchase serves a purpose and enhances your practice in meaningful ways. Start by focusing on versatile instruments that offer multiple uses. For instance, a singing bowl is often used for meditation but its soothing tones can also accompany yoga sessions or even help lull you to sleep. By choosing tools that can serve various functions, you get more bang for your buck, allowing you to explore different aspects of sound healing without needing a separate tool for each one.

Prioritizing quality over quantity is another smart strategy. Buying everything at once is tempting, especially when you're excited to begin your practice. But consider this: A few high-quality instruments will likely serve you better in the long run than a collection of cheaper, less effective ones.

Quality instruments enhance your healing experiences with clearer sound, and they also tend to be more durable, saving you money on replacements down the road. When making a purchase, take your time to research brands and materials, read reviews, and test the instruments in person. A well-crafted tool will be your trusty companion for years, growing with you as your practice evolves.

Timing your purchases can also make a world of difference in maximizing your budget. Keep an eye out for sales, discounts, and holiday promotions. Many retailers offer significant savings during these times, allowing you to stretch your dollar further. Sign up for newsletters from your favorite stores or follow them on social media to stay in the loop about upcoming deals. Planning your purchases around these events can help you build your collection without overspending. It's a little like playing chess—thinking a few moves ahead can lead to a winning strategy.

Beyond instruments, investing in skill-building opportunities is invaluable. Knowledge and expertise are just as important as the tools you use. Attending affordable workshops or online courses can deepen your understanding of sound healing techniques and open new doors in your practice. Look for local events or online platforms offering courses at various prices. Books and resources for self-study are also excellent investments. They provide a wealth of information and inspiration, allowing you to learn at your own pace and revisit topics as needed. Building a solid foundation of knowledge empowers you to make informed decisions about your practice and adapt it to your personal needs and goals.

It's important to regularly assess the impact of your sound healing investments. Keep a log of your expenses and the benefits you've gained from each purchase. This practice keeps you on budget and provides insights into what works best for you. Maybe that singing bowl has become your go-to for winding down after a long day, or perhaps a particular workshop sparked a new interest in sound therapy techniques.

Reflecting on these experiences can help you adjust your investment strategies to align with your evolving practice and personal growth. This ongoing evaluation ensures that your resources are used effectively, helping you get the most out of your sound healing journey.

As we wrap up this chapter, remember that your sound healing practice should resonate with you, both literally and figuratively. By investing wisely, you can build a toolkit that supports your well-being and enhances your daily life. Each choice you make, from versatile instruments to the wealth of knowledge gained through workshops and self-study, contributes to a richer, more fulfilling sound healing experience. In the next chapter, we'll discuss the importance of sustainability and ethics in sound healing, exploring how conscious choices can positively impact both you and the world around you.

Chapter 10

SUSTAINABILITY AND ETHICS IN SOUND HEALING

The ability of music to soothe and restore is one of its great gifts to humanity.

–UNKNOWN

WHEN SHOPPING FOR YOUR sound healing instruments, you might wonder about their past journey before reaching your hands. This curiosity is the first step toward understanding the importance of ethically sourced instruments in sound healing. These tools do more than create harmonious sounds—they carry the weight of their production's impact on the world. As a sound healing practitioner, it's crucial to consider this impact, ensuring that your practice aligns with healing intentions and ethical integrity.

Ethically sourced sound healing instruments play a vital role in preserving the integrity of our beloved practice. When we choose instruments made with care and respect for the Earth, we honor not just our own healing journey but also the ecosystems that nurtured these tools. Unsustainable harvesting practices can disrupt the balance that supports biodiversity, harming delicate ecosystems and, ultimately, our planet's health. For example, overharvesting certain woods for instrument manufacturing can lead to deforestation, which in turn affects countless species and ecosystems. By prioritizing ethical sourcing, we help protect these environments and ensure our healing practices cause no harm.

Fair trade practices are another crucial aspect of ethical sourcing. When instruments are produced under fair trade conditions, the artisans and workers who craft them receive fair wages and work under safe conditions. This supports the well-being of these individuals and their communities and fosters a more equitable global economy. By choosing fair trade instruments, you're investing in a system that values people over profit. This creates a ripple effect of positive change, contributing to a more just world where every hand that touches an instrument is treated with dignity and respect.

When evaluating the ethical sourcing of instruments, look for certain indicators of responsible production. Certifications like Fair Trade or Forest Stewardship Council (FSC) signal sustainable production practices, guaranteeing that the materials used are responsibly sourced and the production methods are environmentally friendly. Transparency in the supply chain is also important. You should be able to trace the journey of your instrument, from raw material to finished product. This transparency builds trust and assures you that your purchase aligns with your values.

Several companies and artisans are committed to ethical production, offering sound healing tools that are both beautiful and responsibly made. Brands like Sound Healing LAB are known for their dedication to sustainability, using recycled materials in their instrument crafting. They offer a wide variety of high-quality sound healing tools, each carefully tested by certified sound healers to ensure effectiveness and integrity. Supporting such brands benefits your practice and encourages the growth of ethical businesses in the sound healing community.

Prioritizing ethical considerations in your purchases can have a profound impact on both your practice and the world. By choosing quality over convenience, you support the artisans and communities that produce these instruments. Opt for instruments crafted by local artisans whenever possible, as this helps strengthen community bonds and reduces the carbon footprint associated with shipping products long distances. Investing in ethically sourced instruments makes you part of a larger movement toward a more sustainable and conscious sound healing practice. This choice enhances your practice's quality and contributes to a healthier planet and a more equitable world.

Reflection Section: Ethical Sound Healing

- **Consider your impact:** Reflect on how your purchasing choices affect the environment and communities.

- **Research brands:** Look for companies known for their ethical and sustainable practices, such as Sound Healing LAB.

- **Support local:** Whenever possible, choose instruments crafted by local artisans to support the community and reduce environmental impact.

- **Share your knowledge:** Educate others in your sound healing community about the importance of ethical sourcing.

As you progress on your sound healing journey, keep in mind that every decision you make—whether selecting instruments or shaping your interactions—reflects your dedication to healing, not only for yourself but also for the world and its inhabitants.

Sustainability in Sound Healing: Eco-Friendly Practices

You've likely heard the word "sustainability" tossed around in various contexts, but what does it mean for sound healing? At its core, sustainable sound healing practice means being mindful of how our actions affect the environment and striving to minimize harm. This involves everything from the materials we choose to how we use and dispose of our instruments. We focus on reducing waste and ensuring that our practices leave a gentle footprint on the Earth. By crafting a space where sound heals the spirit and respects the world, we create alignment and harmony both inside and outside ourselves.

One simple way to incorporate eco-friendly practices into sound healing is by using natural materials for soundproofing and acoustics. Instead of relying on synthetic options, consider using wool, cotton, or even cork to create a sound-friendly environment. These materials absorb sound effectively while adding a touch of warmth and comfort to your space. They're biodegradable, meaning they won't contribute to the growing problem of waste.

Additionally, think about energy efficiency when setting up your sound therapy sessions. Use LED lights to illuminate your space, as they consume less power and last longer than traditional bulbs. If you're using electronic devices for your practice, consider rechargeable batteries or solar-powered options to further reduce energy consumption. These small changes can significantly minimize your environmental impact over time.

Incorporating sustainable practices into sound healing doesn't just protect the planet; it also enhances the quality of your practice. Natural materials, for example, often provide long-term health benefits, as they're less likely to emit harmful chemicals into your environment. This leads to a cleaner, more pleasant space, allowing you to focus on the healing process without distractions.

Sustainable practices also encourage mindfulness, making you more aware of your choices and their broader implications. This awareness can deepen your connection to your practice, reinforcing the idea that healing extends beyond the self to contribute to the well-being of the world.

Communities can play a significant role in promoting sustainability in sound healing. Organizing instrument recycling programs is one way to start. For example, a community event where people come together to recycle old instruments and repurpose materials into new creations is a fun and creative way to extend the life of materials that might otherwise have ended up as waste. Additionally, consider encouraging your sound healing circles to participate in community clean-up events. Organizing a group to clean a local park or beach, followed by a sound healing session, brings people together for a cause bigger than themselves. It offers a chance to connect with others, share practices, and foster a sense of collective responsibility for our environment.

Sustainable sound healing is rooted in mindful choices. Every aspect, from the materials you use to how you bring people together, offers a chance to honor nature and embrace eco-friendly practices. By doing so, you not only enhance your practice but also contribute to a healthier planet. This holistic approach ensures that your vibrations resonate positively, leaving a lasting impact beyond your immediate surroundings.

Cultural Sensitivity: Respecting the Origins of Sound Healing Practices

Indigenous communities around the world have long used sound as a powerful tool for healing and spiritual connection. For the Aboriginal people of Australia, the didgeridoo is more than an instrument; it's a link to their ancestors and the stories of the land.

Similarly, in Tibet, the singing bowl is not just a source of relaxation but a sacred instrument used in meditation and rituals. These practices have deep roots, carrying the wisdom and beliefs of generations past. They remind us that sound healing is a practice steeped in history and cultural significance.

Respecting these cultural traditions is crucial when engaging with sound healing practices. It involves acknowledging the origins and the people who have kept these traditions alive for centuries. Cultural appropriation, which occurs when one culture adopts elements of another without permission or understanding, can strip these practices of their meaning and reduce them to mere trends.

Engaging with sound healing from various cultures calls for awareness and reverence. Taking the time to understand the origins and deeper meanings behind these practices ensures they are honored authentically. These traditions, more than just methods to adopt, embody rich cultural identities that deserve recognition and respect.

To practice cultural sensitivity, start by educating yourself about the history and significance of the sound healing techniques you wish to explore. This could involve reading books, watching documentaries, or attending lectures. Focus on immersing yourself in the cultural context to gain a deeper understanding of the practice.

Honoring cultural exchange means engaging with respect and mutual understanding. This includes obtaining permission when needed and approaching new knowledge with curiosity and humility. Learning directly from cultural practitioners, such as attending their workshops or sessions, helps preserve traditions while offering a deeper, more authentic experience.

Recognizing and respecting the origins of sound healing practices goes beyond personal education; it also means actively contributing to efforts that preserve and uphold these cultural traditions. This could mean donating to organizations that work to protect and promote Indigenous cultures or participating in events that celebrate these traditions.

By doing so, you contribute to the survival and flourishing of these cultures, ensuring that future generations can continue to share in their beauty and wisdom. Attending workshops led by native practitioners enriches your understanding and shows respect for the source culture. These experiences offer invaluable insights into the cultural nuances of the practice, allowing you to engage with sound healing in an informed and respectful way.

Incorporating these respectful practices into your sound healing journey allows you to connect more deeply with the traditions you borrow from. It builds a bridge between your world and theirs, one that is rooted in mutual respect and understanding. Let these principles guide you toward a sound healing practice that heals within while honoring the cultures that have so generously shared their wisdom.

Sound Healing and Global Impact: Contributing to a Healthier World

Though sound healing starts with personal growth and tranquility, it has the potential to ripple outwards, touching lives across the globe. In communities plagued by conflict, where trauma lingers long after the dust settles, sound healing offers hope. Imagine a group of individuals, each carrying their own burdens, gathered in a circle while the gentle vibrations of a singing bowl resonate through the air.

This simple act can help soothe fractured spirits and foster a sense of unity. In war-torn areas, sound therapists work tirelessly to provide relief, using sound to create safe spaces where healing can begin. These practices support mental health by offering a nonintrusive way to process emotions and traumas that words alone can't reach.

Organizations around the world are leveraging sound healing to promote social good. Nonprofits are integrating sound therapy into disaster relief efforts to provide emotional support to those affected. When homes are lost and lives are shattered, the calming presence of sound can offer a moment of peace amidst the chaos.

Programs targeting underserved communities also use sound healing to bridge gaps in mental health care. These initiatives make sound therapy accessible to those who might otherwise lack the resources, ensuring that healing isn't just for the privileged few. By bringing sound healing to those in need, these organizations are making a profound impact, one soothing note at a time.

Getting involved in global sound healing initiatives is easier than you might think. Volunteering with organizations that promote sound healing can be a rewarding way to contribute. Whether it's helping organize community events or assisting in sound therapy sessions, your efforts can make a difference.

Donations are another way to support causes that integrate sound healing into their missions. Even small contributions can help fund programs that bring healing to marginalized communities. These acts of kindness help sustain efforts to spread the benefits of sound healing far and wide, reaching those who need it most.

Sound healing holds immense potential for strengthening global connections. International festivals and events dedicated to sound healing draw people from all walks of life, creating a rich cultural exchange. These events promote unity and an understanding of how sound transcends language and borders. They also provide a platform for learning and collaboration, where attendees can experience the diverse ways sound is used for healing. Through these global gatherings, sound healing becomes a bridge, connecting people and cultures in a shared pursuit of wellness.

Sound healing has the power to effect change on a global scale, through its ability to heal trauma, promote mental health, and bridge cultural divides. By participating in initiatives that use sound for social good, you become part of a larger movement that seeks to spread healing and harmony across the globe. Whether through volunteering, donating, or attending international events, your involvement helps amplify the positive impact of sound healing, making the world a little more peaceful, one vibration at a time.

Future Directions: The Evolving Landscape of Sound Healing

Virtual reality (VR) is set to revolutionize sound therapy by creating immersive environments that deepen relaxation and enhance healing. With a pair of virtual reality goggles, you step into a serene forest where the gentle rustling of leaves blends harmoniously with the soft tones of a distant flute. Though this may sound like a daydream, it's the future of sound healing.

By simulating natural soundscapes or creating entirely new auditory worlds, VR can elevate the therapeutic experience, making it more engaging and effective. A VR setting fully envelopes you in a three-dimensional soundscape that responds to your movements and breathing. This technology holds the potential to bring the soothing effects of sound healing into the homes of those who may not have access to traditional practices.

But the innovation doesn't stop there. Artificial intelligence (AI) is also making waves in sound healing, with the potential to personalize therapy sessions like never before. AI is being developed to analyze your emotional and physical state and select the perfect sound frequencies to address your needs.

AI could tailor sound therapy sessions in real time, adapting to your responses and providing the most effective treatment. This level of personalization could revolutionize how we approach sound healing, making it more precise and impactful. Technology can deepen the connection between sound and well-being, ensuring each session is uniquely suited to the individual.

Ongoing research continues to uncover exciting possibilities for sound healing. Scientists are researching how sound affects genetic expression, exploring the idea that certain frequencies might influence our genes. This research could open new pathways for understanding how sound promotes health at a cellular level, offering insights into its potential for preventing or treating various conditions. This fascinating frontier underscores sound healing's evolution beyond traditional boundaries, integrating with scientific advancements to create more comprehensive health solutions.

Staying informed about these developments is crucial for anyone interested in sound healing. Subscribing to journals and publications dedicated to sound therapy can keep you updated on the latest research and innovations. Attending conferences and symposia focused on future trends is another excellent way to engage with the evolving landscape. These gatherings offer opportunities to learn from experts, network with fellow enthusiasts, and explore new technologies firsthand. By immersing yourself in these resources, you can ensure your practice remains dynamic and informed.

The community's role in shaping the future of sound healing cannot be overstated. Collaborative projects between scientists and practitioners are pivotal in driving innovation. These groups can combine practical experience with scientific inquiry, leading to groundbreaking discoveries. Community-driven research initiatives also play a vital role, allowing individuals to contribute to the collective understanding of sound healing. Whether through grassroots studies or larger collaborative efforts, these initiatives harness the power of community to propel the field forward.

As we conclude this chapter, it's clear that sound healing is poised for an exciting future. The integration of technology, ongoing research, and community collaboration point toward a landscape rich with potential. As these innovations unfold, they promise to enhance personal well-being and contribute to broader societal benefits, bridging gaps and fostering connections.

CONCLUSION

WOW, WHAT A JOURNEY we've been on together! From the first page to the last, we've explored the incredible, far-reaching potential of sound healing. It's been an honor to guide you through this adventure, sharing the wisdom and techniques that have transformed my own life.

We started by laying the foundation, investigating the ancient roots of sound healing and the science behind its effects on the mind and body. Remember those fascinating insights into neuroplasticity and sound's ability to literally reshape our brains? That was just the beginning of the revelations we uncovered.

As we ventured further, we discovered the wide array of instruments and tools at our disposal, from the mesmerizing tones of singing bowls to the precise frequencies of tuning forks. We learned how to create sound sanctuaries and immersive sound bath rituals, infusing our daily lives with moments of peace and clarity.

But this journey didn't just involve external tools and techniques. It also focused on personal growth and inner transformation. Through sound meditation and introspective practices, we explored the landscape of our minds and emotions, learning to harness the power of sound for self-discovery and healing.

We also tackled practical challenges, like finding affordable resources and integrating sound healing into a busy modern lifestyle. We debunked myths and built credibility, empowering ourselves with the knowledge and confidence to share this incredible practice with others.

And that's the real magic of sound healing—its ability to create ripples of positive change that extend far beyond ourselves. By embracing sustainable and ethical practices, we discovered how our individual choices can contribute to a healthier world. We explored the role of community and the joy of connecting with like-minded souls on this path of healing and growth.

So, my friend, here we are at the end of this particular chapter, but really, it's just the beginning of your own sound healing story. I encourage you to integrate the insights and techniques you've learned into your daily life. Experiment with different instruments, create your own rituals, and most importantly, trust in the wisdom of your own body and intuition.

Remember, this practice is a lifelong journey of discovery and adaptation. Stay curious, stay open, and never stop learning. Seek out new workshops, connect with local and online communities, and let your own experiences be your greatest teacher.

As you go forward, know that you are part of a global community of sound healers working together to create a more harmonious and vibrant world. Your voice, your presence, and your unique gifts are all part of this beautiful symphony.

So, keep shining your light, exploring the depths of your own being, and sharing the magic of sound with all you meet. The world needs your healing energy now more than ever.

Thank you, from the bottom of my heart, for joining me on this incredible journey. It's been an absolute joy to share my passion for sound healing with you. May your path to sound healing be filled with many new friends and adventures.

Trust in the power of sound, trust in the wisdom of your own being, and trust in the incredible opportunities that lie ahead.

Here's to the next chapter of your sound healing story, and to the beautiful unfolding of your own unique song.

With love and gratitude,
Grace Bailey

Keeping the Wisdom Alive

Now that you have all the sound healing techniques you need to manage stress, rebuild resilience, and nurture a deeper connection to your body, it's time to pass on your newfound knowledge and help other readers discover the same support and guidance.

If you gained insight from this book, I would appreciate your honest review on Amazon. You'll show other readers seeking healing and growth where they can find the tools they need. Together, we can pass on our passion for Sound Therapy and make it accessible to more people.

Thank you for your support. Sound Therapy thrives when we share what we've learned and experienced—and by leaving your review, you're helping me to do just that.

Scan the QR code or visit the link below to leave your review on Amazon:

http://amazon.com/Body-Wisdom-Through-Sound-Therapy-eboo
k/dp/B0F6GPJQH9

REFERENCES

Yoga for Harmony- Founder, Julie Potter *Singing bowls – Their history and their usage.* https://www.yogaforharmony.co.uk/resources-learning/singing-bowls-their-history-and-their-usage/.

WebMD. (n.d.). *Binaural beats: What are they and what are the benefits?* https://www.webmd.com/balance/what-are-binaural-beats. Medically Reviewed by Carmelita Swiner, MD on April 30, 2023. Written by https://www.webmd.com/bio/webmd-editorial-contributors.

BetterSleep. December 16, 2019. *The science behind Solfeggio frequencies.* https://www.bettersleep.com/blog/science-behind-solfeggio-frequencies.

Five Wellbeing Studio + Spa By Betsy Abrams, January 17, 2023. *Discover the benefits of sound resonance therapy.* https://fivewellbeing.com/discover-the-benefits-of-sound-resonance-therapy/.

Goldsby, T. L., Goldsby, M. E., McWalters, M., & Mills, P. J. (2017). Effects of singing bowl sound meditation on mood, tension, and well-being: An observational study. *Journal of Evidence-Based Integrative Medicine, 22*(4), 401–406. https://doi.org/10.1177/2156587216668109.

Herholz, S. C., & Zatorre, R. J. (2012). Musical training as a framework for brain plasticity: Behavior, function, and structure. *Neuron, 76*(3), 486–502. https://www.ncbi.nlm.nih.gov/pmc/articles/PMC7613141/.

Sound Therapy International. (2018, December 18). *Rehabilitating the nervous system with sound therapy.* https://mysoundtherapy.com/au/2018/12/18/rehabilitating-the-nervous-system-with-sound-therapy/.

Matsuhashi, T., Shimohama, S., & Okamoto, H. (2018). Influence of various intensities of 528 Hz sound-wave in reducing stress levels in rats. *Journal of Interdisciplinary Histopathology, 6*(3), 54–60. https://pubmed.ncbi.nlm.nih.gov/30414050/.

Shanti Bowl. Updated 2025. *How to choose a singing bowl: Complete guide (updated).* https://www.shantibowl.com/blogs/blog/how-to-choose-a-singing-bowl

Academy of Sound Healing. August 01, 2022. *How to use tuning forks for healing | SHA blog.* https://www.academyofsoundhealing.com/blog/how-to-use-tuning-forks-for-healing.

Open Access Government. Modified 19th February, 2025. *Mental health research: The healing power of indigenous drumming.*
https://www.openaccessgovernment.org/article/mental-health-research-the-healing-power-of-indigenous-drumming/188768/

Yoga Anytime. August 19, 2022. *The healing science of crystal singing bowls w Kara.* https://www.yogaanytime.com/blog/lifestyle/the-healing-science-of-crystal-singing-bowls-w-kara

Academy of Sound Healing. (2025). *Free online sound healing course – Sound heals stress.* https://www.academyofsoundhealing.com/free-online-sound-healing-course-sound-heals-stress

Sound Healing Lab. (January 9, 2023). *Creating a sound healing space at home: Tips and tricks.*
https://soundhealinglab.com/blogs/stories/create-sound-healing-space-at-home

Sir Hotels. (n.d.). *How to do a sound bath at home.*
https://www.sirhotels.com/en/blog/how-do-sound-bath-home/

Ollihess. (May 11, 2023) *Rituals with sound: Use your gong every day.* https://www.ollihess.de/en/blogs/blog/rituals-with-sound

Psychology Today. Marlynn Wei, M.D., J.D. (2019, July 24). *The healing power of sound as meditation.*
https://www.psychologytoday.com/us/blog/urban-survival/201907/the-healing-power-of-sound-as-meditation

Metro. Vicki-Marie Cossar, (2023, February 15). *Good vibrations: How sound therapy aids wellbeing and emotional health.*
https://metro.co.uk/2023/02/15/good-vibrations-how-sound-therapy-aids-wellbeing-and-emotional-health-18283431/

Royal Musical Association. (2022, June 14). *Creating nature soundscapes for relaxation.* https://www.rma.ac.uk/2022/06/14/creating-nature-soundscapes-for-relaxation/

Healthline. (August 28, 2024). *Do binaural beats have health benefits?* https://www.healthline.com/health/binaural-beats

Goldsby, T. L., Goldsby, M. E., McWalters, M., & Mills, P. J. (2017). *Effects of singing bowl sound meditation on mood, tension, and well-being: An observational study. Journal of Evidence-Based Integrative Medicine, 22*(4), 401–406.
https://pmc.ncbi.nlm.nih.gov/articles/PMC5871151/

Sound Healers Collective. (n.d.). *The top 3 myths about sound healing: Debunked.* https://soundhealers.net/sound-healing-myths-debunked/

National Center for Complementary and Integrative Health. (n.d.). *Finding and evaluating online resources.*
https://www.nccih.nih.gov/health/finding-and-evaluating-online-resources

Emerge Guided Healing. (2024, December 4). *My sound healing journey: How vibrations transformed my life.*
https://emergeguidedhealing.com/2024/12/04/sound-healing-journey/

Verywell Mind. (2023). *I tried Insight Timer app in 2023, here's how it went.* https://www.verywellmind.com/i-tried-insight-timer-app-review-7724595

Olympic Behavioral Health. (January 8, 2025). *Sound healing: How it works, types, benefits, applications.* https://olympicbehavioralhealth.com/rehab-blog/sound-healing-therapy/

Didge Project. (October 23, 2024). *Facilitate sound baths and sound healing sessions with these 20 instruments.*

https://www.didgeproject.com/artists/facilitate-sound-baths-and-sound-healing-sessions-with-these-20-instruments/

Business Traveler. (2024, September 24). *Six Senses adds sound healing to its global wellness offering*. https://www.businesstraveller.com/business-travel/2024/09/24/six-senses-adds-sound-healing-to-its-global-wellness-offering/

Academy of Sound Healing. (July 29, 2024). *How our sound healing workshops foster strong bonds*. https://www.academyofsoundhealing.com/blog/how-our-sound-healing-workshops-foster-strong-community-bonds

The Ohm Store. (April 12, 2024). *How to create a sound bath: A guide to facilitating for friends and clients*. https://www.theohmstore.co/blogs/our-stories/how-to-create-a-sound-bath-a-guide-to-facilitating-for-friends-and-clients

Inner Sounds Meditation. (n.d.). *On-demand sound healing platform*. https://www.innersoundsmeditation.com/digital-sound-healing-platform

Menla Retreat. (n.d.). *Sound healing immersion retreat*. https://menla.org/retreat/sound-healing-immersion-retreat-2/

Heart and Harmony Music Therapy. (January 29, 2021). *DIY music therapy instruments on a budget*. https://www.heartandharmony.com/diy-music-therapy-instruments/

Sound Healing Greece. (June 24, 2024). *26 sound healing instruments for sound therapy and relaxation*. https://www.soundhealing.gr/20-sound-healing-instruments-for-sound-therapy-and-relaxation/

Academy of Sound Healing. (n.d.). *Free online sound healing courses*. https://www.academyofsoundhealing.com/free-sound-healing-online-courses

Sound Healing Lab. (n.d.). *What makes your store unique?* https://help.soundhealinglab.com/article/21-what-makes-your-store-unique

LinkedIn. (August 8, 2023). *How the world of sound healing is going green*. https://www.linkedin.com/pulse/sustainable-soundscapes-how-world-sound-healing

SoundWell Music Therapy. (April 26, 2019). *Sound practices: Music therapy and culturally competent care*. https://soundwellmusictherapy.com/music-therapy-as-a-culturally-competent-practice/

Global Wellness Institute. (2023, July 7). *Sound wellness initiative trends for 2023*. https://globalwellnessinstitute.org/global-wellness-institute-blog/2023/07/07/sound-wellness-initiative-trends-for-2023/

Yamamoto, T., Ohkuwa, T., Itoh, H., Kitano, T., Terasawa, J., Tsuda, T., & Nakamura, M. (2020). *Physiological effects of 528 Hz sound on the endocrine system and autonomic nervous system*. Journal of Sound and Vibration, 489, 115694. https://doi.org/10.1016/j.jsv.2020.115694

International Pain Foundation. (October 27, 2024). *The healing power of sound therapy for pain relief*. https://internationalpain.org/the-healing-power-of-sound-therapy-for-pain-relief/

National Center for Complementary and Integrative Health. (n.d.). *National Center for Complementary and Integrative Health*. U.S. Department of Health and Human Services, National Institutes of Health. https://www.nccih.nih.gov/

www.ingramcontent.com/pod-product-compliance
Lightning Source LLC
Chambersburg PA
CBHW081006120626
46546CB00010B/3032